THREE FORMS OF UNITY

The Belgic Confession
The Heidelberg Catechism
The Canons of Dort

Ichthus Publications

The text for this reprint edition has been extracted from the 1919 publication of Philip Schaff's *The Creed's of Christendom*, published in New York by Harper & Brothers.

Our goal is to provide high-quality, thought-provoking books that foster encouragement and spiritual growth. For more information regarding bulk purchases, other IP books, or our publishing services, visit us online or write to support@ichthuspublications.com.

Printed in the United States of America.

ISBN: 979-8-9865090-6-8

www.ichthuspublications.com

Contents

ONE

An Introduction to the Belgic Confession ✠ 1

The Belgic Confession (1561) ✠ 9

Article 1: Of the Nature of God | 9
Article 2: Of the Knowledge of God | 9
Article 3: Of Holy Scripture |10
Article 4: Of the Canonical Books of the Old and New Testaments | 10
Article 5: Of the Authority of Holy Scripture | 11
Article 6: Of the Difference Between the Canonical and Apocryphal Books | 12
Article 7: Of the Perfection of Holy Scripture | 12
Article 8: Of the Holy Trinity of Persons in One Divine Essence | 13
Article 9: Of the Scripture Testimony of the Holy Trinity | 14
Article 10: Of the Eternal Deity of the Son of God, Our Lord Jesus Christ | 16
Article 11: Of the Person and Eternal Deity of the Holy Spirit | 17
Article 12: Of the Creation of the World and of the Angels | 17
Article 13: Of the Providence of God | 18
Article 14: Of the Creation, Fall and Corruption of Man |19
Article 15: Of Original Sin | 21
Article 16: Of Divine Predestination | 21
Article 17: Of the Restoration of Natural Man Through the Son of God | 22

Article 18: Of the Incarnation of the Son of God | 22
Article 19: Of the Hypostatic Union, or of the Two Natures in the Person of Christ | 24
Article 20: Of the Means of Redemption Through the Declaration of Justice and Mercy of God in Christ | 25
Article 21: Of the Satisfaction of Christ for Our Sins |25
Article 22: Of Justifying Faith and the Justification of Faith |26
Article 23: Of the Justice by Which We Stand Before God | 27
Article 24: Of Sanctification and of Good Works |28
Article 25: Of the Abolishing of the Ceremonial Law | 29
Article 26: Of Christ's Intercession | 30
Article 27: Of the Catholic Church | 32
Article 28: Of the Communion of the Saints in the True Church | 33
Article 29: Of the Marks of the True Church | 34
Article 30: Of the Government of the Church | 35
Article 31: Of the Calling of Ministers in the Church | 36
Article 32: Of the Power of the Church in Establishing Ecclesiastical Laws and in Administering Discipline |37
Article 33: Of the Sacraments | 37
Article 34: Of Baptism | 38
Article 35: Of the Lord's Supper | 40
Article 36: Of the Magistrate | 42
Article 37: Of the Last Judgment, Resurrection of the Body, and Eternal Life | 43

TWO

An Introduction to the Heidelberg Catechism ✠ 47

The Heidelberg Catechism (1563) ✠ 77

THREE

An Introduction to the Canons of Dort ✠ 123

The Canons of Dort (1618–1619) ✠ 131

First Head of Doctrine: Of Divine Predestination | 131
Second Head of Doctrine: Of the Death of Christ and the Redemption of Men Thereby | 143
Third & Fourth Heads of Doctrine: Of the Corruption of Man, His Conversion to God, and the Manner Thereof | 149
Fifth Head of Doctrine: Of the Perseverance of the Saints | 160

An Introduction to the Belgic Confession[1]

The Reformation in the Netherlands

The Low Countries, conquered from the sea by indomitable energy—the land of Erasmus, of free cities, of inventions, and flourishing commerce—was flooded, through merchants, soldiers, and books, with Protestant ideas from Germany and France, as with waters from the Rhine and the Meuse. Already in 1521 Charles V—who afterwards regretted that he had not burned Luther at Worms—issued from that city an edict for the suppression of heresy in this the most valuable of his inherited dominions. To Belgium belongs the honor of having furnished the first martyrs of evangelical Protestantism in Hendrik Vos and Jan van Essen, two Augustinian monks, who were burned at the stake in Brussels, July 1, 1523, reciting the Apostles' Creed and singing the *Te Deum,* and who were celebrated by Luther in a stirring hymn.[2] This was the fiery signal of a fearful persecution, which reached its height under Philip II of Spain, and the executor of his bloody

[1] All introductions to each of the three forms of unity have been extracted from Philip Schaff, *Creeds of Christendom: With a History and Critical Notes,* Vol. I. "The History of the Creeds," Sixth Ed. (New York: Harper & Brothers, 1919). Footnotes cited have similarly been extracted from the 1919 edition.

[2] See a part of it, in English and German, quoted by Gieseler, Vol. IV. p. 311 (Am. ed.).

designs, the Duke of Alva, but resulted at last in the establishment of national independence and of the Reformed Church in a large part of the Netherlands.

The number of her martyrs exceeds that of any other Protestant Church during the sixteenth century and perhaps that of the whole primitive Church under the Roman Empire.[3] During the ever-memorable conflict under William of Orange, who was assassinated by a fanatical papist in 1584, and his second son Maurice—an able military commander and strict Calvinist (d. 1625)—the Bible, with the Belgic Confession and Heidelberg Catechism, was the spiritual guide and comforter of the Protestants and fortified them against the assaults of the enemy. Calvinism, which fears God and nobody else, inspired that heroic courage which triumphed over the political and religious despotism of Spain and raised Holland to an extraordinary degree of commercial and literary eminence.[4]

Guido de Brès

The chief author of the Belgic Confession is Guido (or Guy, Wido) de Brès, a noble evangelist and martyr of the Reformed Church of the Netherlands. He was born about 1523 at Mons in

[3] Grotius estimates the number of Protestant martyrs in Holland, under one reign, at one hundred thousand. Gibbon (*History of the Decline*, etc., at the close of ch. XVI) confidently asserts that "the number of Protestants who were executed by the Spaniards in a single province and a single reign, far exceeded that of the primitive martyrs in the space of three centuries, and of the Roman empire." And Motley (*History of the Rise of the Dutch Republic*, Vol. II. p. 504) says of the terrible reign of Alva: "The barbarities committed amid the sack and ruin of those blazing and starving cities are almost beyond belief; unborn infants were torn from the living bodies of their mothers; women and children were violated by the thousands, and whole populations burned and hacked to pieces by soldiers in every mode which cruelty in its wanton ingenuity could devise."

[4] It is strange that Motley, in his great works on the Rise, and the History of the Dutch Republic, ignores the Belgic Confession, and barely mentions the name of Guido de Brès.

Hennegau, educated in the Roman Church, and by diligent reading of the Scriptures, converted to the evangelical faith. Expelled from his country, he sought refuge in London under Edward VI where he joined the Belgic fugitives and prepared himself for the ministry. Afterwards, he studied at Lausanne and became a traveling evangelist in southwestern Belgium and northern France—from Dieppe to Sedan, from Valenciennes to Antwerp. After the conquest of French Flanders, he was, together with the younger missionary from Geneva, Pérégrin de la Grange, taken prisoner, put in chains, and hanged on the last day of May, 1567 for disobedience to the commands of the court at Brussels and especially for the distribution of the holy communion in the Reformed congregations. From prison, the youthful martyr wrote letters of comfort to his brethren, his old mother, his wife, and his children and met his death as if it were a marriage-feast.[5] In his proper home, Protestantism was completely suppressed, but in the neighboring countries of Holland and the Lower Rhine, it spread and flourished.

The Belgic Confession

The Belgic Confession was prepared in 1561 by Guido de Brès, with the aid of Adrien de Saravia (professor of theology in Leyden, afterwards at Cambridge, where he died, 1613), H. Modetus (for some time chaplain of William of Orange), and Godfrey Wingen, in the French language, to prove the Reformed faith from the Word of God.[6] It was revised by Francis Junius of

[5] See, on Guy de Brès, the enlarged edition of Crespin's *Histoire des Martyrs*, Genève, 1617, pp. 731–750, and the Brussels edition of the *Conf. de foi*, p. 19.

[6] Saravia, in a letter to Uytenbogardus (Apr. 13, 1612), quoted by Niemeyer (Proleg. p. lii.) and Gieseler (*Ch. Hist.* Vol. IV. p. 314, Am. ed.), says: "*Ego me illius confessionis ex primis unum fuisse auctoribus profiteor, sicut et Hermannus Modetus: nescio an plures sint superstites. Illa primo fuit*

Bourges (1545–1602)—a student of Calvin, pastor of a Walloon congregation at Antwerp, and afterwards professor of theology at Leyden—who abridged the sixteenth article and sent a copy to Geneva and other churches for approval. It was probably printed in 1562, or at all events in 1566, and afterwards translated into Dutch, German, and Latin. It was presented to the bigoted Philip II, 1562, in the vain hope of securing toleration and with an address which breathes the genuine spirit of martyrdom. The petitioners protest against the charge of being rebels and declare that notwithstanding, they number more than a hundred thousand and are exposed to the most cruel oppression; they obey the Government in all lawful things; but that rather than deny Christ before men, they would "offer their backs to stripes, their tongues to knives, their mouths to gags, and their whole bodies to the fire, well knowing that those who follow Christ must take his cross and deny themselves."[7]

The Confession was publicly adopted by a Synod at Antwerp (1566), then at Wesel (1568), more formally by a Synod at Emden (1571)[8] by a national Synod at Dort (1574), another at Middelburg (1581), and again by the great Synod of Dort, April 29, 1619. But inasmuch as the Arminians had demanded partial changes, and the text had become confused, the Synod of Dort submitted the French, Latin, and Dutch texts to a careful revision.

conscripta Gallico sermone a Christi servo et martyre Guidone de Brès, sed antequam ederetur ministris verbi Dei, quos potuit nancisci, illam communicavit: et emendandum si quid displiceret, addendum, detrahendum proposuit, ut unius opus censeri non debeat. Sed nemo eorum, qui manum apposuerunt, umquam cogitavit fidei canonem edere, verum ex canonicis scriptis fidem suam probare." Editor's Note: Nicolaas H. Gootjes concludes these men were only "consultants rather than co-authors," *The Belgic Confession: Its History and Sources* (Grand Rapids, MI: Baker, 2007), 36.

[7] The address is given in full by Böckel, l.c. pp. 480–484.

[8] The Brussels ed. (p. viii.) says: "*Le 8 Octobre, en 1571, il fût statué par le premier synode national des Églises wallonnes et flamandes ténu à Embden, que cette Confession serait signée par tous les membres présents au dit synode et par tous ceux qui seraient admis au saint ministère.*"

Since that time the Belgic Confession, together with the Heidelberg Catechism, has been the recognized symbol of the Reformed Churches in Holland and Belgium.[9] It is also the doctrinal standard of the Reformed (Dutch) Church in America, which holds to it even more tenaciously than the mother Church in the Netherlands.[10]

Contents

The Belgic Confession contains thirty-seven Articles and follows the order of the Gallican Confession, but is less polemical and more full and elaborate: especially on the Trinity, the Incarnation, the Church, and the Sacraments.[11] It is, upon the whole, the best symbolical statement of the Calvinistic system of doctrine, with the exception of the Westminster Confession.

[9] The *Société évangélique* or *Église Chrétienne missionnaire belge* requires from its ministers a qualified subscription to the Belgic Confession with "*une réserve préalable en repoussant ce qui dans la Confession belge regarde l'exercise du pouvoir civil en matière de foi.*"

[10] The following formula of subscription is required from ministers of the Dutch Reformed Church in America: "We, the underwritten, Ministers of the Word of God, residing within the bounds of the Classis of N. N., do hereby sincerely, and in good conscience before the Lord, declare by this our subscription, that we heartily believe, and are persuaded, that all the articles and points of doctrine contained in the [Belgic] Confession and [Heidelberg] Catechism of the Reformed [Dutch] Church, together with the explanation of some points of the aforesaid doctrine made in the National Synod held at Dordrecht, in the year 1619, do fully agree with the Word of God. We promise, therefore, diligently to teach, and faithfully to defend the aforesaid doctrine, without either directly or indirectly contradicting the same by our public preaching or writings. We declare, moreover, that we not only reject all errors that militate against this doctrine, and particularly those which are condemned in the above-mentioned Synod, but that we are disposed to refute and contradict them, and to exert ourselves in keeping the Church pure from such errors. And if hereafter any difficulties or different sentiments respecting the aforesaid doctrine should arise in our minds, we promise that we will neither publicly nor privately propose, teach, or defend the same, either by preaching or by writing, until we have first revealed such sentiment to the Consistory, Classis, or Synod, that the same may be there examined," etc.

[11] Ebrard (*Handbuch der Kirchen-und Dogmengesch.* Vol. III. p. 319) says that besides the Gallican Confession as the basis, use was made also of the Friesian Confession of Utenhoven, which the English exiles brought with them to Emden, and of the Catechism of Laski.

The Text

The text has undergone several modifications as regards the wording and length, but not as regards the doctrine.

The French text must be considered as the original.[12] Of the first edition of 1561 or 1562, no copies are known. The Synod of Antwerp, in September 1580, ordered a precise parchment copy of the revised text (of Junius) to be made for its archives, which copy had to be signed by every new minister. This manuscript has always been regarded in the Belgic churches as the authentic document.[13] The Synod of Dort ordered a new revision with a view to bring the Latin, French, and Dutch texts into harmony on the basis of the manuscript copy of 1580. The Leyden edition of 1669 gives in two parallel columns the original text and the revised text of Dort. A Rotterdam edition of the Psalter, 1787, carefully reprints the original text in the old spelling from the manuscript, with the changes of Dort in notes. The Brussels edition of 1850 presents the ancient text of 1580, as revised at Dort, in modern French.[14]

Next in authority is the Latin text, but of this there are likewise several recensions: a shorter and a larger. The first Latin translation was made from the revised French copy of Francis Janius,

[12] It is entitled, "*Confession de Foy faicte d'un commun accord pour les fidèles qui conversent ès Pays-Bas, lesquels désirent vivre selon la pureté de l'Évangile de nostre Seigneur Jésus-Christ.*" This title is followed by two mottoes—the one from Apoc. ii. 10: "*Sois fidèle jusques à la mort et je te donneray la couronne de vie;*" the other from 1 Pet. iii. 15: "*Soyez tousjours appareillez à respondre à chacun qui vous demande raison de l'espérance qui est en vous.*" On the second leaf, there is over the head of the first article the brief title, "*Confession vrayement Chrétienne contenant le sommaire de la doctrine de Dieu et salut éternel de l'âme.*"

[13] The Brussels ed. says (p. 39): "*C'est probablement d'après la copie de Junius que cette Confession a été imprimée dans le livre des Martyrs de Crespin. Le text de Crespin ne diffère pas de celui du manuscrit authentique.*"

[14] This careful edition, issued by the Evangelical Society of Belgium, is reproduced in the third volume of *Creeds of Christendom*, together with the English version now used by the Dutch Reformed Church in America. Both agree, sentence for sentence.

probably by Beza, or under his direction, for the *Harmonia Confessionum*, Geneva, 1581 (distributed under different heads, with the other Confessions).[15] The same passed into the first edition of the *Corpus et Syntagma Confessionum*, Geneva, 1612. Another translation was prepared, 1618, for the use of the Synod of Dort, by Festus Hommius, pastor in Leyden, and one of the scribes of that Synod.[16] This text was revised in the following year by that Synod and thus approved and incorporated with its acts in the 146th session.[17] The revision of Dort was reproduced in the second edition of the *Corpus et Syntagma Conf.*, 1654.[18] The excellent English version in use in the Reformed Dutch Church of America is made from the Latin text of the Synod of Dort.

[15] See *Note critique* at the close of the Brussels edition, p. 39: "*Junius envoya une copie de cette révision à Genève. Theodore de Beza la fit imprimer* [*in French?*]. *C'est lui, sans doute, qui la traduisit en latin, comme elle se trouve dans 'l'Harmonia Confessionum,' Genevæ*, 1581." That this was the first Latin translation is stated in the *Harmonia*, p. 3: "*Belgica, Gallice omnium Belgicarum Ecclesiarum nomine anno* 1566 *edita, ac demum anno* 1579 [1571?] *in publica Belgii Synodo repetita et confirmata, Belgiceque versa. Nunc denique a nobis etiam Latine expressa.*"

[16] "*Confessio ecclesiarum reformatarum in Belgio. . . . in usum futuræ synodi nationalis latine edidit et collegit Festus Hommius.*" Ludg. Batav. 1618. Niemeyer (pp. 360 sqq.) gives this translation, which more nearly agrees with the older version, and he adds some readings from the first edition of the *Corpus et Syntagma*.

[17] See the extracts from the Acts of the 144th Session, April 29, 1619, in Niemeyer, p. lv.

[18] Under the title *Ecclesiarum Belgicarum Christiana atque Orthodoxa Confessio, summam doctrinæ de Deo et æterna animarum salute complectens, prout in Synodo Dortrechtana fuit recognita et approbata*. The articles are numbered, but have no titles. The difference between this and the first Latin translation may be judged from the following specimen: Harmonia Confessionum, 1581 (p. 36). Corpus et Syntagma Confessionum, ed. II., 1654 (p. 129). Art. I. *Corde credimus, et ore confitemur, unicam esse et simplicem essentiam spiritualem, quam Deum vocamus, æternum, incomprehensibilem, inconspicuum, immutabilem, infinitum, qui totus est sapiens, fonsque omnium bonorum uberrimus*. Art. I. *Corde credimus, et ore confitemur* OMNES, *unicam esse et simplicem essentiam spiritualem, quam Deum vocamus,* EUMQUE *æternum, incomprehensibilem, invisibilem, infinitum,* OMNIPOTENTEM, SUMME SAPIENTEM, JUSTUM ET BONUM, *omniumque bonorum fontem uberrimum*.

The Belgic Confession
(1561)

Article 1: Of the Nature of God

We all believe with the heart and confess with the mouth[1] that there is only one God,[2] who is a simple and spiritual Being;[3] He is eternal,[4] incomprehensible,[5] invisible,[6] immutable,[7] infinite,[8] almighty,[9] perfectly wise,[10] just,[11] good,[12] and the overflowing fountain of all good.[13]

[1] Rom 10:10 [2] Deut 6:4; 1 Cor 8:4, 6; 1 Tim 2:5 [3] Jn 4:24 [4] Ps 90:2 [5] Rom 11:33 [6] Col 1:15; 1 Tim 6:16 [7] Jas 1:17 [8] 1 Kings 8:27; Jer 23:24 [9] Gen 17:1; Mt 19:26; Rev 1:8 [10] Rom 16:27 [11] Rom 3:25, 26; Rom 9:14; Rev 16:5, 7 [12] Mt 19:17 [13] Jas 1:17

Article 2: Of the Knowledge of God

We know Him by two means: First, by the creation, preservation, and government of the universe; which is before our eyes as a most beautiful book,[1] wherein all creatures, great and small, are as so many letters leading us to perceive clearly the invisible things of God, namely, His eternal power and deity, as the apostle Paul says (Rom 1:20). All these things are sufficient to convict men and leave them without excuse. Second, He makes Himself more clearly and fully known to us by His holy and divine Word[2] as far as is necessary for us in this life, to His glory and our salvation.

[1] Ps 19:1–4 [2] Ps 19:7, 8; 1 Cor 1:18–21

Article 3: Of Holy Scripture

We confess that this Word of God did not come by the impulse of man, but that men moved by the Holy Spirit spoke from God, as the apostle Peter says (2 Pet 1:21). Thereafter, in His special care for us and our salvation, God commanded His servants, the prophets and apostles, to commit His revealed Word to writing[1] and He Himself wrote with His own finger the two tables of the law.[2] Therefore we call such writings holy and divine Scriptures.[3]

[1] Ex 34:27; Ps 102:18; Rev 1:11, 19 [2] Ex 31:18 [3] 2 Tim 3:16

Article 4: Of the Canonical Books of the Old and New Testaments

We believe that the Holy Scriptures consist of two parts, namely, the Old and the New Testament, which are canonical, against which nothing can be alleged. These books are listed in the church of God as follows:

> THE BOOKS OF THE OLD TESTAMENT: the five books of Moses, namely, Genesis, Exodus, Leviticus, Numbers, Deuteronomy; Joshua, Judges, Ruth, 1 and 2 Samuel, 1 and 2 Kings, 1 and 2 Chronicles, Ezra, Nehemiah, Esther; Job, Psalms, Proverbs, Ecclesiastes, the Song of Songs; Isaiah, Jeremiah,

Lamentations, Ezekiel, Daniel, Hosea, Joel, Amos, Obadiah, Jonah, Micah, Nahum, Habakkuk, Zephaniah, Haggai, Zechariah, and Malachi.

THE BOOKS OF THE NEW TESTAMENT: the four gospels, namely, Matthew, Mark, Luke, and John; the Acts of the Apostles; the thirteen letters of the apostle Paul, namely, Romans, 1 and 2 Corinthians, Galatians, Ephesians, Philippians, Colossians, 1 and 2 Thessalonians, 1 and 2 Timothy, Titus, Philemon; the letter to the Hebrews; the seven other letters, namely, James, 1 and 2 Peter, 1, 2 and 3 John, Jude; and the Revelation to the apostle John.

Article 5: Of the Authority of Holy Scripture

We receive[1] all these books, and these only, as holy and canonical, for the regulation, foundation, and confirmation of our faith.[2] We believe without any doubt all things contained in them, not so much because the church receives and approves them as such, but especially because the Holy Spirit witnesses in our hearts that they are from God,[3] and also because they contain the evidence thereof in themselves; for, even the blind are able to perceive that the things foretold in them are being fulfilled.[4]

[1] 1 Thess 2:13. [2] 2 Tim 3:16, 17. [3] 1 Cor 12:3; 1 Jn 4:6, 1 Jn 5:7. [4] Deut 18:21, 22; 1 Kings 22:28; Jer 28:9; Ezek 33:33

Article 6: Of the Difference Between the Canonical and Apocryphal Books

We distinguish these holy books from the apocryphal, namely, 3 and 4 Esdras, Tobit, Judith, Wisdom, Ecclesiasticus, Baruch, additions to Esther, the Prayer of Azariah and the Song of the Three Young Men in the Furnace, Susannah, Bel and the Dragon, the Prayer of Manasseh, and 1 and 2 Maccabees. The church may read and take instruction from these so far as they agree with the canonical books. They are, however, far from having such power and authority that we may confirm from their testimony any point of faith or of the Christian religion; much less may they be used to detract from the authority of the holy books.

Article 7: Of the Perfection of Holy Scripture

We believe that this Holy Scripture fully contains the will of God and that all that man must believe in order to be saved is sufficiently taught therein.[1] The whole manner of worship which God requires of us is written in it at length. It is therefore unlawful for any one, even for an apostle, to teach otherwise than we are now taught in Holy Scripture:[2] yes, even if it be an angel from heaven, as the apostle Paul says (Gal 1:8). Since it is forbidden to add to or take away anything from the Word of God (Deut 12:32),[3] it is evident that the doctrine thereof is most perfect and complete in all respects.[4]

We may not consider any writings of men, however holy these men may have been, of equal value with the divine Scriptures; nor ought we to consider custom, or the great multitude, or antiquity, or succession of times and persons, or councils, decrees or statutes, as of equal value with the truth of God, since the truth is above all;[5] for all men are of themselves liars, and lighter than a breath (Ps 62:9). We therefore reject with all our heart whatever does not agree with this infallible rule,[6] as the apostles have taught us: Test the spirits to see whether they are of God (1 Jn 4:1). Likewise: If any one comes to you and does not bring this doctrine, do not receive him into your house or give him any greeting (2 Jn 1:10).

[1] 2 Tim 3:16, 17; 1 Pet 1:10–12. [2] 1 Cor 15:2; 1 Tim 1:3. [3] Deut 4:2; Prov 30:6; Acts 26:22; 1 Cor 4:6; Rev 22:18, 19. [4] Ps 19:7; Jn 15:15; Acts 18:28; Acts 20:27; Rom 15:4. [5] Mk 7:7–9; Acts 4:19; Col 2:8; 1 Jn 2:19. [6] Deut 4:5,6; Is 8:20; 1 Cor 3:11; Eph 4:4–6; 2 Thess 2:2; 2 Tim 3:14, 15

Article 8: Of the Holy Trinity of Persons in One Divine Essence

According to this truth and this Word of God, we believe in one only God,[1] who is one single essence, in which are three persons, really, truly, and eternally distinct according to their incommunicable properties; namely, the Father, the Son, and the Holy Spirit.[2] The Father is the cause, origin, and beginning of all things visible and invisible.[3] The Son is the Word, the wisdom, and the image of the Father.[4] The Holy Spirit is the eternal power and might who proceeds from the Father and the Son.[5] Nevertheless, God is not by this distinction divided into three, since the Holy Scriptures teach us that the Father, the Son, and the Holy Spirit each has His personal existence, distinguished by Their properties; but in such a way that these three persons are but one only God.

It is therefore evident that the Father is not the Son, nor the Son the Father, and likewise the Holy Spirit is neither the Father nor the Son. Nevertheless, these persons thus distinguished are not divided, nor intermixed; for the Father has not assumed our flesh and blood, neither has the Holy Spirit, but the Son only. The Father has never been without His Son,[6] or without His Holy Spirit. For these three, in one and the same essence, are equal in eternity. There is neither first nor last; for They are all three one, in truth, in power, in goodness, and in mercy.

[1] 1 Cor 8:4–6. [2] Mt 3:16, 17; Mt 28:19. [3] Eph 3:14, 15. [4] Prov 8:22–31; Jn 1:14; Jn 5:17–26; 1 Cor 1:24; Col 1:15–20; Heb 1:3; Rev 19:13. [5] Jn 15:26. [6] Mic 5:2; Jn 1:1, 2.

Article 9: Of the Scripture Testimony of the Holy Trinity

All this we know both from the testimonies of Holy Scripture[1] and from the respective works of the three Persons, and especially those we perceive in ourselves. The testimonies of Scripture which lead us to believe this Holy Trinity are written in many places of the Old Testament. It is not necessary to mention them all; it is sufficient to select some with discretion.

In the book of Genesis God says: "Let Us make man in our image after our likeness . . . So God created man in His own image . . . ; male and female He created them" (Gen 1:26, 27). Also: "Behold, the man has become like one of Us" (Gen 3:22). From God's saying, "Let Us make man in Our image," it appears that there are more divine persons than one; and when He says, "God created," He indicates that there is one God. It is true, He does not say how many persons there are, but what seems to be somewhat obscure in the Old Testament is very plain in the New Testament. For when our Lord was baptized in the river Jordan, the voice of the Father was heard, who said, "This is My beloved Son" (Mt 3:17); the Son was seen in the water, and the Holy Spirit descended upon Him in bodily form as a dove.[2] For the baptism of all believers, Christ prescribed this formula: "Baptize all nations into the Name of the Father, and of the Son, and of the Holy Spirit" (Mt 28:19). In the gospel according to Luke, the angel Gabriel thus addressed Mary, the mother of our Lord: "The Holy Spirit will come upon you, and the power of the Most High will overshadow you; therefore the child to be born will be called holy, the Son of God" (Luke 1:35). Likewise: "The grace of the Lord Jesus Christ and the love of God and the fellowship of the Holy Spirit be with you all" (2 Cor 13:14). In all these places we are fully taught that there are three persons in one only divine essence.

Although this doctrine far surpasses all human understanding, nevertheless in this life we believe it on the ground of the Word of God, and we expect to enjoy its perfect knowledge and fruit hereafter in heaven.

Moreover, we must observe the distinct offices and works of these three Persons towards us. The Father is called our Creator by His power; the Son is our Saviour and Redeemer by His blood; the Holy Spirit is our Sanctifier by His dwelling in our hearts. The doctrine of the Holy Trinity has always been maintained and preserved in the true church since the time of the apostles to this very day, over against Jews, Muslims, and against false Christians and heretics such as Marcion, Mani, Praxeas, Sabellius, Paul of Samosata, Arius, and such like, who have been justly condemned by the orthodox fathers. In this doctrine, therefore, we willingly receive the three creeds, of the Apostles, of Nicaea, and of Athanasius; likewise, that which in accordance with them is agreed upon by the early fathers.

[1] Jn 14:16; Jn 15:26; Acts 2:32, 33; Rom 8:9; Gal 4:6; Tit 3:4–6; 1 Pet 1:2; 1 Jn 4:13, 14; 1 Jn 5:1–12; Jude 20, 21; Rev 1:4, 5. [2] Mt 3:16.

Article 10: Of the Eternal Deity of the Son of God, Our Lord Jesus Christ

We believe that Jesus Christ according to His divine nature is the only-begotten Son of God,[1] begotten from eternity, not made, nor created—for then He would be a creature—but of the same essence with the Father, equally-eternal, who reflects the glory of God and bears the very stamp of His nature (Heb 1:3), and is equal to Him in all things.[2] He is the Son of God, not only from the time that He assumed our nature but from all eternity, [3] as these testimonies, when compared with each other, teach us: Moses says that God created the world;[4] the apostle John says that all things were made by the Word which he calls God.[5] The letter to the Hebrews says that God made the world through His Son;[6] likewise the apostle Paul says that God created all things through Jesus Christ. [7] Therefore, it must necessarily follow that He who is called God, the Word, the Son, and Jesus Christ, did exist at that time when all things were created by Him. Therefore, He could say, "Truly, I say to you, before Abraham was, I am" (Jn 8:58), and He prayed, "Glorify Thou Me in Thy own presence with the glory which I had with Thee before the world was made" (Jn 17:5). And so, He is true, eternal God, the Almighty, whom we invoke, worship, and serve.

[1] Mt 17:5; Jn 1:14, 18; Jn 3:16; Jn 14:1–14; Jn 20:17, 31; Rom 1:4; Gal 4:4; Heb 1:2; [2] Jn 5:18, 23; Jn 10:30; Jn 14:9; Jn 20:28; Rom 9:5; Phil 2:6; Col 1:15; Tit 2:13; [3] Jn 8:58; Jn 17:5; Heb 13:8. [4] Gen 1:1. [5] Jn 1:1–3. [6] Heb 1:2. [7] 1 Cor 8:6; Col 1:16.

Article 11: Of the Person and Eternal Deity of the Holy Spirit

We believe and confess also that the Holy Spirit from eternity proceeds from the Father and the Son. He is neither made, created, nor begotten, but He can only be said to proceed from both.[1] In order He is the third Person of the Holy Trinity, of one and the same essence, majesty, and glory with the Father and the Son, true and eternal God, as the Holy Scriptures teach us.[2]

[1] Jn 14:15–26; Jn 15:26; Rom 8:9. [2] Gen 1:2; Mt 28:19; Acts 5:3, 4; 1 Cor 2:10; 1 Cor 3:16; 1 Cor 6:11; 1 Jn 5:7.

Article 12: Of the Creation of the World and of the Angels

We believe that the Father through the Word, that is, through His Son, has created out of nothing heaven and earth and all creatures, when it seemed good to Him,[1] and that He has given to every creature its being, shape, and form, and to each its specific task and function to serve its Creator. We believe that He also continues to sustain and govern them according to His eternal providence and by His infinite power in order to serve man, to the end that man may serve his God.

He also created the angels good, to be His messengers and to serve His elect.[2] Some of these have fallen from the exalted position in which God created them into everlasting perdition,[3] but the others have by the grace of God remained steadfast and continued in their first state. The devils and evil spirits are so depraved that they are enemies of God and of all that is good.[4] With all their might, they lie in wait like murderers to ruin the church and all its members and to destroy everything by their wicked devices.[5] They are therefore by their own wickedness sentenced to eternal damnation and daily expect their horrible torments.[6]

Therefore, we detest and reject the error of the Sadducees, who deny that there are any spirits and angels;[7] and also the error of the Manichees, who say that the devils were not created, but have their origin of themselves, and that without having become corrupted, they are wicked by their own nature.

[1] Gen 1:1; Gen 2:3; Is 40:26; Jer 32:17; Col 1:15, 16; 1 Tim 4:3; Heb 11:3; Rev 4:11. [2] Ps 103:20, 21; Mt 4:11; Heb 1:14. [3] Jn 8:44; 2 Pet 2:4; Jude 6. [4] Gen 3:1–5; 1 Pet 5:8. [5] Eph 6:12; Rev 12:4, 13–17; Rev 20:7–9. [6] Mt 8:29; Mt 25:41; Rev 20:10. [7] Acts 23:8.

Article 13: Of the Providence of God

We believe that this good God, after He had created all things, did not abandon them or give them up to fortune or chance,[1] but that according to His holy will He so rules and governs them that in this world nothing happens without His direction.[2] Yet God is not the Author of the sins which are committed nor can He be charged with them.[3] For His power and goodness are so great and beyond understanding that He ordains and executes His work in the most excellent and just manner, even when devils and wicked men act unjustly.[4] And as to His actions surpassing human understanding, we will not curiously inquire farther than our capacity allows us. But with the greatest humility and reverence we adore the just judgments of God, which are hidden from us,[5] and we content ourselves that we are pupils of Christ, who have only to learn those things which He teaches us in His Word, without transgressing these limits.[6]

This doctrine gives us unspeakable consolation, for we learn thereby that nothing can happen to us by chance, but only by the direction of our gracious heavenly Father. He watches over us with fatherly care, keeping all creatures so under His power that not one hair of our head—for they are all numbered—nor one sparrow can fall to the ground without the will of our Father (Mt 10:29, 30). In this we trust, because we know that He holds in check the devil and all our enemies so that they cannot hurt us without His permission and will.[7]

We therefore reject the damnable error of the Epicureans, who say that God does not concern Himself with anything but leaves all things to chance.

[1] Jn 5:17; Heb 1:3. [2] Ps 115:3; Prov 16:1, 9, 33; Prov 21:1; Eph 1:11, 12; Jas 4:13–15. [3] Jas 1:13; 1 Jn 2:16. [4] Job 1:21; Is 10:5; Is 45:7; Amos 3:6; Acts 2:23; Acts 4:27, 28. [5] 1 Kings 22:19–23; Rom 1:28; 2 Thess 2:11. [6] Deut 29:29; 1 Cor 4:6. [7] Gen 45:8; Gen 50:20; 2 Sam 16:10; Rom 8:28, 38, 39.

Article 14: Of the Creation, Fall and Corruption of Man

We believe that God created man of dust from the ground[1] and He made and formed him after His own image and likeness, good, righteous, and holy.[2] His will could conform to the will of God in every respect. But, when man was in this high position, he did not appreciate it nor did he value his excellency. He gave ear to the words of the devil and willfully subjected himself to sin and consequently to death and the curse.[3] For he transgressed the commandment of life which he had received; by his sin he broke away from God, who was his true life; he corrupted his whole nature. By all this he made himself liable to physical and spiritual death.[4]

Since man became wicked and perverse, corrupt in all his ways, he has lost all his excellent gifts which he had once received from God.[5] He has nothing left but some small traces, which are sufficient to make man inexcusable.[6] For whatever light is in us has changed into darkness,[7] as Scripture teaches us, "The light shines in the darkness, and the darkness has not overcome it" (Jn 1:5); where the apostle John calls mankind darkness.

Therefore, we reject all teaching contrary to this concerning the free will of man, since man is but a slave to sin (Jn 8:34) and no one can receive anything except what is given him from heaven (Jn 3:27). For who dares to boast that he of himself can do any good, when Christ says: "No one can come to Me unless the Father who sent Me draws him" (Jn 6:44)? Who will glory in his own will when he understands that the mind that is set on the flesh is hostile to God (Rom 8:7)? Who can speak of his knowledge, since the unspiritual man does not receive the gifts of the Spirit of God (1 Cor 2:14)? In short, who dares to claim anything when he realizes that we are not competent of ourselves to claim anything as coming from us, but that our competence is from God (2 Cor 3:5)? Therefore, what the apostle says must justly remain sure and firm: "God is at work in you both to will and to work for His good pleasure" (Phil 2:13). For there is no understanding nor will conformable to the understanding and will of God unless Christ has brought it about; as He teaches us: "Apart from Me you can do nothing" (Jn 15:5).

[1] Gen 2:7; Gen 3:19; Eccles 12:7. [2] Gen 1:26, 27; Eph 4:24; Col 3:10. [3] Gen 3:16–19; Rom 5:12. [4] Gen 2:17; Eph 2:1; Eph 4:18. [5] Ps 94:11; Rom 3:10; Rom 8:6. [6] Rom 1:20, 21. [7] Eph 5:8.

Article 15: Of Original Sin

We believe that by the disobedience of Adam original sin has spread throughout the whole human race.[1] It is a corruption of the entire nature of man[2] and a hereditary evil which infects even infants in their mother's womb.[3] As a root it produces in man all sorts of sin. It is, therefore, so vile and abominable in the sight of God that it is sufficient to condemn the human race.[4] It is not abolished nor eradicated even by baptism, for sin continually streams forth like water welling up from this woeful source.[5] Yet, in spite of all this, original sin is not imputed to the children of God to their condemnation, but by His grace and mercy is forgiven them.[6] This does not mean that the believers may sleep peacefully in their sin, but that the awareness of this corruption may make them often groan as they eagerly wait to be delivered from this body of death.

In this regard, we reject the error of the Pelagians who say that this sin is only a matter of imitation.

[1] Rom 5:12–14, 19. [2] Rom 3:10. [3] Job 14:4; Ps 51:5; Jn 3:6. [4] Eph 2:3. [5] Rom 7:18, 19. [6] Eph 2:4, 5.

Article 16: Of Divine Predestination

We believe that when the entire offspring of Adam plunged into perdition and ruin by the transgression of the first man,[1] God manifested Himself to be as He is: merciful and just. Merciful, in rescuing and saving from this perdition those whom in His eternal and unchangeable counsel[2] He has elected[3] in Jesus Christ our Lord[4] by His pure goodness, without any consideration of their works.[5] Just, in leaving the others in the fall and perdition into which they have plunged themselves.[6]

[1] Rom 3:12. [2] Jn 6:37, 44; Jn 10:29; Jn 17:2, 9, 12; Jn 18:9. [3] 1 Sam 12:22; Ps 65:4; Acts 13:48; Rom 9:16; Rom 11:5; Tit 1:1. [4] Jn 15:16, 19; Rom 8:29; Eph 1:4, 5. [5] Mal 1:2, 3; Rom 9:11–13; 2 Tim 1:9; Tit 3:4, 5. [6] Rom 9:19–22; 1 Pet 2:8.

Article 17: Of the Restoration of Natural Man Through the Son of God

We believe that, when He saw that man had thus plunged himself into physical and spiritual death and made himself completely miserable, our gracious God in His marvelous wisdom and goodness set out to seek man when he trembling fled from Him.[1] He comforted him with the promise that He would give him His Son, born of woman (Gal 4:4), to bruise the head of the serpent (Gen 3:15) and to make man blessed.[2]

[1] Gen 3:9. [2] Gen 22:18; Is 7:14; Jn 1:14; Jn 5:46; Jn 7:42; Acts 13:32, 33; Rom 1:2, 3; Gal 3:16;

Article 18: Of the Incarnation of the Son of God

We confess, therefore, that God has fulfilled the promise He made to the fathers by the mouth of His holy prophets[1] when, at the time appointed by Him,[2] He sent into the world His own only-begotten and eternal Son, who took the form of a servant and was born in the likeness of men (Phil 2:7). He truly assumed a real human nature with all its infirmities,[3] without sin,[4] for He was conceived in the womb of the blessed virgin Mary by the power of the Holy Spirit and not by the act of a man.[5] He not only assumed human nature as to the body, but also a true human soul, in order that He might be a real man. For since the soul was lost as well as the body, it was necessary that He should assume both to save both.

Contrary to the heresy of the Anabaptists, who deny that Christ assumed human flesh of His mother, we therefore confess that Christ partook of the flesh and blood of the children (Heb 2:14). He is a fruit of the loins of David (Acts 2:30); born of the seed of David according to the flesh (Rom 1:3); a fruit of the womb of the virgin Mary (Luke 1:42); born of woman (Gal 4:4); a branch of David (Jer 33:15); a shoot from the stump of Jesse (Is 11:1); sprung from the tribe of Judah (Heb 7:14); descended from the Jews according to the flesh (Rom 9:5); of the seed of Abraham(Gal 3:16), since the Son was concerned with the descendants of Abraham. Therefore, He had to be made like His brethren in every respect, yet without sin (Heb 2:16, 17; Heb 4:15).

In this way He is in truth our Immanuel, that is, God with us (Mt 1:23).

[1] Gen 26:4; 2 Sam 7:12–16; Ps 132:11; Lk 1:55; Acts 13:23. [2] Gal 4:4. [3] 1 Tim 2:5; 1 Tim 3:16; Heb 2:14. [4] 2 Cor 5:21; Heb 7:26; 1 Pet 2:22. [5] Mt 1:18; Lk 1:35.

Article 19: Of the Hypostatic Union, or of the Two Natures in the Person of Christ

We believe that by this conception the person of the Son of God is inseparably united and joined with the human nature,[1] so that there are not two sons of God, nor two persons, but two natures united in one single person. Each nature retains its own distinct properties: His divine nature has always remained uncreated, without beginning of days or end of life (Heb 7:3), filling heaven and earth.[2] His human nature has not lost its properties; it has beginning of days and remains created. It is finite and retains all the properties of a true body.[3] Even though, by His resurrection, He has given immortality to His human nature, He has not changed its reality,[4] since our salvation and resurrection also depend on the reality of His body.[5]

However, these two natures are so closely united in one person that they were not even separated by His death. Therefore, what He, when dying, committed into the hands of His Father was a real human spirit that departed from His body.[6] Meanwhile, His divinity always remained united with His human nature, even when He was lying in the grave.[7] And the divine nature always remained in Him just as it was in Him when He was a little child, even though it did not manifest itself as such for a little while.

For this reason, we profess Him to be true God and true man: true God in order to conquer death by His power; and true man that He might die for us according to the infirmity of His flesh.

[1] Jn 1:14; Jn 10:30; Rom 9:5; Phil 2:6, 7. [2] Mt 28:20. [3] 1 Tim 2:5. [4] Mt 26:11; Lk 24:39; Jn 20:25; Acts 1:3, 11; Acts 3:21; Heb 2:9. [5] 1 Cor 15:21; Phil 3:21. [6] Mt 27:50. [7] Rom 1:4.

Article 20: Of the Means of Redemption Through the Declaration of Justice and Mercy of God in Christ

We believe that God, who is perfectly merciful and just, sent His Son to assume that nature in which disobedience had been committed,[1] to make satisfaction in that same nature; and to bear the punishment of sin by His most bitter passion and death.[2] God therefore manifested His justice against His Son when He laid our iniquity on Him[3] and poured out His goodness and mercy on us, who were guilty and worthy of damnation. Out of a most perfect love, He gave His Son to die for us, and He raised Him for our justification[4] that through Him we might obtain immortality and life eternal.

[1] Rom 8:3. [2] Heb 2:14. [3] Rom 3:25, 26; Rom 8:32. [4] Rom 4:25.

Article 21: Of the Satisfaction of Christ for Our Sins

We believe that Jesus Christ was confirmed by an oath to be a High Priest forever, after the order of Melchizedek.[1] He presented Himself in our place before His Father, appeasing God's wrath by His full satisfaction,[2] offering Himself on the tree of the cross, where He poured out His precious blood to purge away our sins,[3] as the prophets had foretold.[4] For it is written, Upon Him was the chastisement that made us whole and with His stripes we are healed.[5] Like a lamb He was led to the slaughter. He was numbered with the transgressors (Is 53:5, 7, 12),[6] and condemned as a criminal by Pontius Pilate, though he had first declared Him innocent.[7] He restored what He had not stolen (Ps 69:4). He died as the righteous for the unrighteous (1 Pet

3:18).[8] He suffered in body and soul,[9] feeling the horrible punishment caused by our sins, and His sweat became like great drops of blood falling down upon the ground (Luke 22:44). Finally, He exclaimed, "My God, My God, why hast Thou forsaken Me" (Mt 27:46)? All this He endured for the forgiveness of our sins.

Therefore, we justly say, with Paul, that we know nothing except Jesus Christ and Him crucified (1 Cor 2:2). We count everything as loss because of the surpassing worth of knowing Jesus our Lord (Phil 3:8). We find comfort in His wounds and have no need to seek or invent any other means of reconciliation with God than this only sacrifice, once offered, by which the believers are perfected for all times (Heb 10:14).[10] This is also the reason why the angel of God called Him Jesus, that is, Saviour, because He would save His people from their sins (Mt 1:21).[11]

[1] Ps 110:4; Heb 7:15–17. [2] Rom 4:25; Rom 5:8, 9; Rom 8:32; Gal 3:13; Col 2:14; Heb 2:9, 17; Heb 9:11–15. [3] Acts 2:23; Phil 2:8; 1 Tim 1:15; Heb 9:22; 1 Pet 1:18, 19; 1 Jn 1:7; Rev 7:14. [4] Lk 24:25–27; Rom 3:21; 1 Cor 15:3. [5] 1 Pet 2:24. [6] Mk 15:28. [7] Jn 18:38. [8] Rom 5:6. [9] Ps 22:15. [10] Heb 7:26–28; Heb 9:24–28. [11] Lk 1:31; Acts 4:12.

Article 22: Of Justifying Faith and the Justification of Faith

We believe that, in order that we may obtain the true knowledge of this great mystery, the Holy Spirit kindles in our hearts a true faith.[1] This faith embraces Jesus Christ with all His merits, makes Him our own, and does not seek anything besides Him.[2] For it must necessarily follow, either that all we need for our salvation is not in Jesus Christ or, if it is all in Him, that one who has Jesus Christ through faith, has complete salvation.[3] It is, therefore, a terrible blasphemy to assert that Christ is not sufficient, but that something else is needed besides Him; for the conclusion would then be that Christ is only half a Saviour.

Therefore, we rightly say with Paul that we are justified by faith alone, or by faith apart from works of law (Rom 3:28).[4] Meanwhile, strictly speaking, we do not mean that faith as such justifies us,[5] for faith is only the instrument by which we embrace Christ our righteousness; He imputes to us all His merits and as many holy works as He has done for us and in our place.[6] Therefore, Jesus Christ is our righteousness, and faith is the instrument that keeps us with Him in the communion of all His benefits. When those benefits have become ours, they are more than sufficient to acquit us of our sins.

[1] Jn 16:14; 1 Cor 2:12; Eph 1:17, 18. [2] Jn 14:6; Acts 4:12; Gal 2:21. [3] Ps 32:1; Mt 1:21; Lk 1:77; Acts 13:38, 39; Rom 8:1. [4] Rom 3:19–4:8; Rom 10:4–11; Gal 2:16; Phil 3:9; Tit 3:5. [5] 1 Cor 4:7. [6] Jer 23:6; Mt 20:28; Rom 8:33; 1 Cor 1:30, 31; 2 Cor 5:21; 1 Jn 4:10.

Article 23: Of the Justice by Which We Stand Before God

We believe that our blessedness lies in the forgiveness of our sins for Jesus Christ's sake and that therein our righteousness before God[1] consists, as David and Paul teach us. They pronounce a blessing upon the man to whom God reckons righteousness apart from works (Rom 4:6; Ps 32:1). The apostle also says that we are justified by His grace as a gift, through the redemption which is in Christ Jesus (Rom 3:24).[2]

Therefore, we always hold to this firm foundation. We give all the glory to God,[3] humble ourselves before Him, and acknowledge ourselves to be what we are. We do not claim anything for ourselves or our merits,[4] but rely and rest on the only obedience of Jesus Christ crucified;[5] His obedience is ours when we believe in Him.[6]

This is sufficient to cover all our iniquities and to give us confidence in drawing near to God, freeing our conscience of fear, terror, and dread, so that we do not follow the example of our first father, Adam, who trembling tried to hide and covered himself with fig leaves.[7] For indeed, if we had to appear before God, relying—be it ever so little—on ourselves or some other creature, (woe be to us!) we would be consumed.[8] Therefore, everyone must say with David, "O LORD, enter not into judgment with Thy servant, for no man living is righteous before Thee" (Ps 143:2).

[1] 1 Jn 2:1. [2] 2 Cor 5:18, 19; Eph 2:8; 1 Tim 2:6. [3] Ps 115:1; Rev 7:10–12. [4] 1 Cor 4:4; Jas 2:10. [5] Acts 4:12; Heb 10:20. [6] Rom 4:23–25. [7] Gen 3:7; Zeph 3:11; Heb 4:16; 1 Jn 4:17–19. [8] Lk 16:15; Phil 3:4–9.

Article 24: Of Sanctification and of Good Works

We believe that this true faith, worked in man by the hearing of God's Word and by the operation of the Holy Spirit,[1] regenerates him and makes him a new man.[2] It makes him live a new life and frees him from the slavery of sin.[3] Therefore, it is not true that this justifying faith makes man indifferent to living a good and holy life.[4] On the contrary, without it no one would ever do anything out of love for God,[5] but only out of self-love or fear of being condemned. It is therefore impossible for this holy faith to be inactive in man, for we do not speak of an empty faith but of what Scripture calls faith working through love (Gal 5:6). This faith induces man to apply himself to those works which God has commanded in His Word. These works, proceeding from the good root of faith, are good and acceptable in the sight of God, since they are all sanctified by His grace. Nevertheless, they do not count toward our justification. For through faith in Christ, we are justified, even before we do any good works.[6] Otherwise, they could not be good any more than the fruit of a tree can be good unless the tree itself is good.[7]

Therefore, we do good works, but not for merit. For what could we merit? We are indebted to God, rather than He to us, for the good works we do,[8] since it is He who is at work in us, both to will and to work for His good pleasure (Phil 2:13). Let us keep in mind what is written: "So you also, when you have done all that is commanded you, say, 'We are unworthy servants; we have only done what was our duty'" (Luke 17:10). Meanwhile, we do not deny that God rewards good works,[9] but it is by His grace that He crowns His gifts.

Furthermore, although we do good works, we do not base our salvation on them. We cannot do a single work that is not defiled by our flesh and does not deserve punishment.[10] Even if we could show one good work, the remembrance of one sin is enough to make God reject it.[11] We would then always be in doubt, tossed to and fro without any certainty, and our poor consciences would be constantly tormented, if they did not rely on the merit of the death and passion of our Saviour.[12]

[1] Acts 16:14; Rom 10:17; 1 Cor 12:3. [2] Ezek 36:26, 27; Jn 1:12, 13; Jn 3:5; Eph 2:4–6; Tit 3:5; 1 Pet 1:23. [3] Jn 5:24; Jn 8:36; Rom 6:4–6; 1 Jn 3:9. [4] Gal 5:22; Tit 2:12. [5] Jn 15:5; Rom 14:23; 1 Tim 1:5; Heb 11:4, 6. [6] Rom 4:5. [7] Mt 7:17. [8] 1 Cor 1:30, 31; 1 Cor 4:7; Eph 2:10. [9] Rom 2:6, 7; 1 Cor 3:14; 2 Jn 8; Rev 2:23. [10] Rom 7:21. [11] Jas 2:10. [12] Hab 2:4; Mt 11:28; Rom 10:11.

Article 25: Of the Abolishing of the Ceremonial Law

We believe that the ceremonies and symbols of the law have ceased with the coming of Christ, and that all shadows have been fulfilled,[1] so that the use of them ought to be abolished among Christians. Yet their truth and substance remain for us in Jesus Christ, in whom they have been fulfilled.[2]

In the meantime, we still use the testimonies taken from the law and the prophets, both to confirm us in the doctrine of the gospel and to order our life in all honor, according to God's will and to His glory.[3]

[1] Mt 27:51; Rom 10:4; Heb 9:9, 10. [2] Mt 5:17; Gal 3:24; Col 2:17. [3] Rom 13:8–10; Rom 15:4; 2 Pet 1:19; 2 Pet 3:2.

Article 26: Of Christ's Intercession

We believe that we have no access to God except through the only Mediator[1] and Advocate, Jesus Christ the righteous.[2] For this purpose, He became man, uniting together the divine and human nature, that we men might not be barred from but have access to the divine majesty.[3] This Mediator, however, whom the Father has ordained between Himself and us, should not frighten us by His greatness, so that we look for another according to our fancy. There is no creature in heaven or on earth who loves us more than Jesus Christ.[4] Though He was in the form of God, He emptied Himself, taking the form of man and of a servant for us (Phil 2:6, 7) and was made like His brethren in every respect (Heb 2:17). If, therefore, we had to look for another intercessor, could we find one who loves us more than He who laid down His life for us, even while we were His enemies (Rom 5:8, 10)? If we had to look for one who has authority and power, who has more than He who is seated at the right hand of the Father[5] and who has all authority in heaven and on earth (Mt

28:18)? Moreover, who will be heard more readily than God's own well-beloved Son?[6]

Therefore, it was pure lack of trust which introduced the custom of dishonoring the saints rather than honoring them, doing what they themselves never did nor required. On the contrary, they constantly rejected such honor according to their duty,[7] as appears from their writings. Here one ought not to bring in our unworthiness, for it is not a question of offering our prayers on the basis of our own worthiness, but only on the basis of the excellence and worthiness of Jesus Christ,[8] whose righteousness is ours by faith.[9]

Therefore, with good reason, to take away from us this foolish fear or rather distrust, the author of Hebrews says to us that Jesus Christ was made like His brethren in every respect, so that He might become a merciful and faithful High Priest in the service of God, to make expiation for the sins of the people. For because He Himself has suffered and been tempted, He is able to help those who are tempted (Heb 2:17, 18). Further, to encourage us more to go to Him, he says: "Since then we have a great High Priest who has passed through the heavens, Jesus, the Son of God, let us hold fast our confession. For we have not a High Priest who is unable to sympathize with our weaknesses, but one who in every respect has been tempted as we are, yet without sin. Let us then with confidence draw near to the throne of grace, that we may receive mercy and find grace to help in time of need" (Heb 4:14–16).[10] The same letter says: "Therefore brethren, since we have confidence to enter the sanctuary by the blood of Jesus . . . let us draw near with a true heart in full assurance of faith," etc. (Heb 10:19, 22). Also, Christ holds His priesthood permanently, because He continues forever. Consequently, He is able for all time to save those who draw near to God through Him, since He always lives to make intercession for them (Heb 7:24, 25).[11] What more is needed? Christ Himself says: "I am the way, and the truth, and the life; no one comes to the Father, but by Me" (Jn 14:6). Why should we look for another advocate? It has pleased God to give us His Son as our Advocate. Let us then not leave Him for another, or even look for another, without ever finding one. For when God gave Him to us, He knew very well that we were sinners.

In conclusion, according to the command of Christ, we call upon the heavenly Father through Christ our only Mediator,[12] as we are taught in the Lord's prayer.[13] We rest assured that we shall obtain all we ask of the Father in His Name (Jn 16:23).[14]

[1] 1 Tim 2:5. [2] 1 Jn 2:1. [3] Eph 3:12. [4] Mt 11:28; Jn 15:13; Eph 3:19; 1 Jn 4:10. [5] Heb 1:3; Heb 8:1. [6] Mt 3:17; Jn 11:42; Eph 1:6. [7] Acts 10:26; Acts 14:15. [8] Jer 17:5, 7; Acts 4:12. [9] 1 Cor 1:30. [10] Jn 10:9; Eph 2:18; Heb 9:24. [11] Rom 8:34. [12] Heb 13:15. [13] Mt 6:9–13; Lk 11:2–4. [14] Jn 14:13.

Article 27: Of the Catholic Church

We believe and profess one catholic or universal church,[1] which is a holy congregation and assembly[2] of the true Christian believers, who expect their entire salvation in Jesus Christ,[3] are washed by His blood, and are sanctified and sealed by the Holy Spirit.[4]

This church has existed from the beginning of the world and will be to the end, for Christ is an eternal King who cannot be without subjects.[5] This holy church is preserved by God against the fury of the whole world,[6] although for a while it may look very small and as extinct in the eyes of man.[7] Thus during the perilous reign of Ahab, the Lord kept for Himself seven thousand persons who had not bowed their knees to Baal.[8]

Moreover, this holy church is not confined or limited to one particular place or to certain persons, but is spread and dispersed throughout the entire world.[9] However, it is joined and united with heart and will, in one and the same Spirit, by the power of faith.[10]

[1] Gen 22:18; Is 49:6; Eph 2:17–19. [2] Ps 111:1; Jn 10:14, 16; Eph 4:3–6; Heb 12:22, 23. [3] Joel 2:32; Acts 2:21. [4] Eph 1:13; Eph 4:30. [5] 2 Sam 7:16; Ps 89:36; Ps 110:4; Mt 28:18, 20; Lk 1:32. [6] Ps 46:5; Mt 16:18. [7] Is 1:9; 1 Pet 3:20; Rev 11:7. [8] 1 Kgs 19:18; Rom 11:4. [9] Mt 23:8; Jn 4:21–23; Rom 10:12, 13. [10] Ps 119:63; Acts 4:32; Eph 4:4.

Article 28: Of the Communion of the Saints in the True Church

We believe, since this holy assembly and congregation is the assembly of the redeemed and there is no salvation outside of it,[1] that no one ought to withdraw from it, content to be by himself, no matter what his status or standing may be. But all and everyone are obliged to join it and unite with it,[2] maintaining the unity of the church. They must submit themselves to its instruction and discipline,[3] bend their necks under the yoke of Jesus Christ,[4] and serve the edification of the brothers and sisters,[5] according to the talents which God has given them as members of the same body.[6]

To observe this more effectively, it is the duty of all believers, according to the Word of God, to separate from those who do not belong to the church[7] and to join this assembly[8] wherever God has established it. They should do so even though the rulers and edicts of princes were against it and death or physical punishment might follow.[9]

All therefore who draw away from the church or fail to join it act contrary to the ordinance of God.

[1] Mt 16:18, 19; Acts 2:47; Gal 4:26; Eph 5:25–27; Heb 2:11, 12; Heb 12:23. [2] 2 Chron 30:8; Jn 17:21; Col 3:15. [3] Heb 13:17. [4] Mt 11:28–30. [5] Eph 4:12. [6] 1 Cor 12:7, 27; Eph 4:16. [7] Num 16:23–26; Is 52:11, 12; Acts 2:40; Rom 16:17; Rev 18:4. [8] Ps 122:1; Is 2:3; Heb 10:25. [9] Acts 4:19, 20.

Article 29: Of the Marks of the True Church

We believe that we ought to discern diligently and very carefully from the Word of God what is the true church, for all sects which are in the world today claim for themselves the name of church.[1] We are not speaking here of the hypocrites, who are mixed in the church along with the good and yet are not part of the church, although they are outwardly in it.[2] We are speaking of the body and the communion of the true church which must be distinguished from all sects that call themselves the church.

The true church is to be recognized by the following marks: It practices the pure preaching of the gospel.[3] It maintains the pure administration of the sacraments as Christ instituted them.[4] It exercises church discipline for correcting and punishing sins.[5] In short, it governs itself according to the pure Word of God,[6] rejecting all things contrary to it[7] and regarding Jesus Christ as the only Head.[8] Hereby the true church can certainly be known and no one has the right to separate from it.

Those who are of the church may be recognized by the marks of Christians. They believe in Jesus Christ the only Saviour,[9] flee from sin and pursue righteousness,[10] love the true God and their neighbour[11] without turning to the right or left, and crucify their flesh and its works.[12] Although great weakness remains in them, they fight against it by the Spirit all the days of their life.[13] They appeal constantly to the blood, suffering, death, and obedience of Jesus Christ, in whom they have forgiveness of their sins through faith in Him.[14]

The false church assigns more authority to itself and its ordinances than to the Word of God. It does not want to submit itself to the yoke of Christ.[15] It does not administer the sacraments as Christ commanded in His Word, but adds to them and subtracts from them as it pleases. It bases itself more on men than on Jesus Christ. It persecutes those who live holy lives according to the Word of God and who rebuke the false church for its sins, greed, and idolatries.[16]

These two churches are easily recognized and distinguished from each other.

[1] Rev 2:9. [2] Rom 9:6. [3] Gal 1:8; 1 Tim 3:15. [4] Acts 19:3–5; 1 Cor 11:20–29. [5] Mt 18:15–17; 1 Cor 5:4, 5, 13; 2 Thess 3:6, 14; Tit 3:10. [6] Jn 8:47; Jn 17:20; Acts 17:11; Eph 2:20; Col 1:23; 1 Tim 6:3. [7] 1 Thess 5:21; 1 Tim 6:20; Rev 2:6. [8] Jn 10:14; Eph 5:23; Col 1:18. [9] Jn 1:12; 1 Jn 4:2. [10] Rom 6:2; Phil 3:12. [11] 1 Jn 4:19–21. [12] Gal 5:24. [13] Rom 7:15; Gal 5:17. [14] Rom 7:24, 25; 1 Jn 1:7–9. [15] Acts 4:17, 18; 2 Tim 4:3, 4; 2 Jn 9. [16] Jn 16:2.

Article 30: Of the Government of the Church

We believe that this true church must be governed according to the Spiritual order which our Lord has taught us in His Word.[1] There should be ministers or pastors to preach the Word of God and to administer the sacraments;[2] there should also be elders[3] and deacons[4] who, together with the pastors, form the council of the church.[5] By these means they preserve the true religion; they see to it that the true doctrine takes its course, that evil men are disciplined in a spiritual way and are restrained, and also that the poor and all the afflicted are helped and comforted according to their need.[6] By these means everything will be done well and in good order when faithful men are chosen[7] in agreement with the rule that the apostle Paul gave to Timothy.[8]

[1] Acts 20:28; Eph 4:11, 12; 1 Tim 3:15; Heb 13:20, 21. [2] Lk 1:2; Lk 10:16; Jn 20:23; Rom 10:14; 1 Cor 4:1; 2 Cor 5:19, 20; 2 Tim 4:2. [3] Acts 14:23; Tit 1:5. [4] 1 Tim 3:8–10. [5] Phil 1:1; 1 Tim 4:14. [6] Acts 6:1–4; Tit 1:7–9. [7] 1 Cor 4:2. [8] 1 Tim 3.

Article 31: Of the Calling of Ministers in the Church

We believe that ministers of God's Word, elders, and deacons ought to be chosen to their offices by lawful election of the church, with prayer and in good order, as stipulated by the Word of God.[1] Therefore, everyone shall take care not to intrude by improper means. He shall wait for the time that he is called by God so that he may have sure testimony and thus be certain that his call comes from the Lord.[2] Ministers of the Word, in whatever place they are, have equal power and authority, for they are all servants of Jesus Christ,[3] the only universal Bishop and the only Head of the church.[4] In order that this holy ordinance of God may not be violated or rejected, we declare that everyone must hold the ministers of the Word and the elders of the church in special esteem because of their work[5] and, as much as possible, be at peace with them without grumbling or arguing.

[1] Acts 1:23, 24; Acts 6:2, 3. [2] Acts 13:2; 1 Cor 12:28; 1 Tim 4:14; 1 Tim 5:22; Heb 5:4. [3] 2 Cor 5:20; 1 Pet 5:1–4. [4] Mt 23:8, 10; Eph 1:22, Eph 5:23. [5] 1 Thess 5:12, 13; 1 Tim 5:17; Heb 13:17.

Article 32: Of the Power of the Church in Establishing Ecclesiastical Laws and in Administering Discipline

We believe that, although it is useful and good for those who govern the church to establish a certain order to maintain the body of the church, they must at all times watch that they do not deviate from what Christ, our only Master, has commanded.[1] Therefore, we reject all human inventions and laws introduced into the worship of God which bind and compel the consciences in any way.[2] We accept only what is proper to preserve and promote harmony and unity and to keep all in obedience to God.[3] To that end, discipline and excommunication ought to be exercised in agreement with the Word of God.[4]

[1] 1 Tim 3:15. [2] Is 29:13; Mt 15:9; Gal 5:1. [3] 1 Cor 14:33. [4] Mt 16:19; Mt 18:15–18; Rom 16:17; 1 Cor 5; 1 Tim 1:20.

Article 33: Of the Sacraments

We believe that our gracious God, mindful of our insensitivity and weakness, has ordained sacraments to seal His promises to us and to be pledges of His good will and grace towards us. He did so to nourish and sustain our faith.[1] He has added these to the Word of the gospel[2] to represent better to our external senses both what He declares to us in His Word and what He does inwardly in our hearts. Thus, He confirms to us the salvation which He imparts to us. Sacraments are visible signs and seals of something internal and invisible, by means of which God works in us through the power of the Holy Spirit.[3] Therefore, the signs are not void and meaningless so that they deceive us. For Jesus Christ is their truth; apart from Him they would be nothing. Moreover, we are satisfied with the number of sacraments which Christ our Master has instituted for us, namely, two: the sacrament of baptism[4] and the holy supper of Jesus Christ.[5]

[1] Gen 17:9–14; Ex 12; Rom 4:11. [2] Mt 28:19; Eph 5:26. [3] Rom 2:28, 29; Col 2:11, 12. [4] Mt 28:19. [5] Mt 26:26–28; 1 Cor 11:23–26.

Article 34: Of Baptism

We believe and confess that Jesus Christ, who is the end of the law (Rom 10:4), has by His shed blood put an end to every other shedding of blood that one could or would make as an expiation or satisfaction for sins. He has abolished circumcision, which involved blood, and has instituted in its place the sacrament of baptism.[1] By baptism we are received into the church of God and set apart from all other peoples and false religions, to be entirely committed to Him[2] whose mark and emblem we bear. This serves as a testimony to us that He will be our God and gracious Father for ever.

For that reason, He has commanded all those who are His to be baptized with plain water, into the Name of the Father and of the Son and of the Holy Spirit (Mt 28:19). By this He signifies to us that as water washes away the dirt of the body when poured on us, and as water is seen on the body of the baptized when sprinkled on him, so the blood of Christ, by the Holy Spirit, does the same thing internally to the soul.[3] It washes and cleanses our soul from sin[4] and regenerates us from children of wrath into children of God.[5] This is not brought about by the water as such[6] but by the sprinkling of the precious blood of the Son of God,[7] which is our Red Sea,[8] through which we must pass to escape the tyranny of Pharaoh, that is, the devil, and enter into the spiritual land of Canaan.

Thus, the ministers on their part give us the sacrament and what is visible, but our Lord gives us what is signified by the sacrament, namely, the invisible gifts and grace. He washes, purges, and cleanses our souls of all filth and unrighteousness,[9] renews our hearts and fills them with all comfort, gives us true assurance of His fatherly goodness, clothes us with the new nature, and takes away the old nature with all its works.[10]

We believe, therefore, that anyone who aspires to eternal life ought to be baptized only once.[11] Baptism should never be repeated, for we cannot be born twice. Moreover, baptism benefits us not only when the water is on us and when we receive it, but throughout our whole life. For that reason, we reject the error of the Anabaptists, who are not content with a single baptism received only once, and who also condemn the baptism of the little children of believers. We believe that these children ought to be baptized and sealed with the sign of the covenant, as infants were circumcised in Israel on the basis of the same promises which are now made to our children.[12] Indeed, Christ shed His blood to wash the children of believers just as much as He shed it for adults.[13] Therefore, they ought to receive the sign and sacrament of what Christ has done for them, as the Lord commanded in the law that a lamb was to be offered shortly after children were born.[14] This was a sacrament of the passion and death of Jesus Christ. Because baptism has the same meaning for our children as circumcision had for the people of Israel, Paul calls baptism the circumcision of Christ (Col 2:11).

[1] Col 2:11. [2] Ex 12:48; 1 Pet 2:9. [3] Mt 3:11; 1 Cor 12:13. [4] Acts 22:16; Heb 9:14; 1 Jn 1:7; Rev 1:5b. [5] Tit 3:5. [6] 1 Pet 3:21. [7] Rom 6:3; 1 Pet 1:2; 1 Pet 2:24. [8] 1 Cor 10:1–4. [9] 1 Cor 6:11; Eph

5:26. [10] Rom 6:4; Gal 3:27. [11] Mt 28:19; Eph 4:5. [12] Gen 17:10–12; Mt 19:14; Acts 2:39. [13] 1 Cor 7:14. [14] Lev 12:6.

Article 35: Of the Lord's Supper

We believe and confess that our Saviour Jesus Christ has instituted the sacrament of the holy supper[1] to nourish and sustain those whom He has already regenerated and incorporated into His family, which is His church.

Those who are born anew have a twofold life.[2] One is physical and temporal, which they received in their first birth and is common to all men. The other is spiritual and heavenly, which is given them in their second birth and is effected by the word of the gospel[3] in the communion of the body of Christ. This life is not common to all, but only to the elect of God.

For the support of the physical and earthly life, God has ordained earthly and material bread. This bread is common to all just as life is common to all. For the support of the spiritual and heavenly life, which believers have, He has sent them a living bread which came down from heaven (Jn 6:51), namely, Jesus Christ,[4] who nourishes and sustains the spiritual life of the believers[5] when He is eaten by them, that is, spiritually appropriated and received by faith.[6]

To represent to us the spiritual and heavenly bread, Christ has instituted earthly and visible bread as a sacrament of His body and wine as a sacrament of His blood.[7] He testifies to us that as certainly as we take and hold the sacrament in our hands and eat and drink it with our mouths, by which our physical life is then sustained, so certainly do we receive by faith,[8] as the hand and mouth of our soul, the true body and true blood of Christ, our only Saviour, in our souls for our spiritual life.

It is beyond any doubt that Jesus Christ did not commend His sacraments to us in vain. Therefore, He works in us all that He represents to us by these holy signs. We do not understand the manner in which this is done, just as we do not comprehend the hidden activity of the Spirit of God.[9] Yet we do not go wrong when we say that what we eat and drink is the true, natural body and the true blood of Christ. However, the manner in which we eat it is not by mouth but in the spirit by faith. In that way, Jesus Christ always remains seated at the right hand of God His Father in heaven;[10] yet He does not cease to communicate Himself to us by faith. This banquet is a spiritual table at which Christ makes us partakers of Himself with all His benefits and gives us the grace to enjoy both Himself and the merit of His suffering and death.[11] He nourishes, strengthens, and comforts our poor, desolate souls by the eating of His flesh and refreshes and renews them by the drinking of His blood.

Although the sacrament is joined together with that which is signified, the latter is not always received by all.[12] The wicked certainly takes the sacrament to his condemnation, but he does not receive the truth of the sacrament. Thus, Judas and Simon the sorcerer both received the sacrament, but they did not receive Christ, who is signified by it.[13] He is communicated exclusively to the believers.[14]

Finally, we receive this holy sacrament in the congregation of the people of God[15] with humility and reverence as we together commemorate the death of Christ our Saviour with thanksgiving, and we confess our faith and Christian religion.[16] Therefore, no one should come to this table without careful self-examination, lest by eating this bread and drinking from this cup, he eat and drink judgment upon himself (1 Cor 11:28, 29). In short, we are moved by the use of this holy sacrament to a fervent love of God and our neighbors. Therefore, we reject as desecrations all additions and damnable inventions which men have mixed with the sacraments. We declare that we should be content with the ordinance taught by Christ and His apostles and should speak about it as they have spoken.

[1] Mt 26:26–28; Mk 14:22–24; Lk 22:19, 20; 1 Cor 11:23–26. [2] Jn 3:5, 6. [3] Jn 5:25. [4] Jn 6:48–51. [5] Jn 6:63; Jn 10:10b. [6] Jn 6:40, 47. [7] Jn 6:55; 1 Cor 10:16. [8] Eph 3:17. [9] Jn 3:8. [10] Mk 16:19; Acts 3:21. [11] Rom 8:32; 1 Cor 10:3, 4. [12] 1 Cor 2:14. [13] Lk 22:21, 22; Acts 8:13, 21. [14] Jn 3:36. [15] Acts 2:42; Acts 20:7. [16] Acts 2:46; 1 Cor 11:26.

Article 36: Of the Magistrate

We believe that, because of the depravity of mankind, our gracious God has ordained kings, princes, and civil officers.[1] He wants the world to be governed by laws and policies,[2] in order that the licentiousness of men be restrained and that everything be conducted among them in good order.[3] For that purpose, He has placed the sword in the hand of the government to punish wrongdoers and to protect those who do what is good (Rom 13:4). Their task of restraining and sustaining is not limited to the public order, but includes the protection of the church and its ministry in order that the [1]kingdom of Christ may come,

[1] The Christian Reformed Church Synod of 1958, in line with 1910 and 1938, substituted the following statement in place of the one indicated, which it judged unbiblical: "And being called in this manner to contribute to the advancement of a society that is pleasing to God, the civil rulers have the task, subject to God's law, of removing every obstacle to the preaching of the gospel and to every aspect of divine worship. They should do this while completely refraining from every tendency towards exercising absolute authority, and while functioning in the sphere entrusted to them, with the means belonging to them. They should do it in order that the Word of God may

the Word of the gospel may be preached everywhere,[4] and God may be honored and served by everyone, as He requires in His Word.

Moreover, everyone—no matter of what quality, condition, or rank—ought to be subject to the civil officers, pay taxes, hold them in honor and respect, and obey them in all things[5] which do not disagree with the Word of God.[6] We ought to pray for them that God may direct them in all their ways and that we may lead a quiet and peaceable life, godly and respectful in every way (1 Tim 2:1, 2).

For that reason, we condemn the Anabaptists and other rebellious people, and in general all those who reject the authorities and civil officers, subvert justice,[7] introduce a communion of goods, and confound the decency that God has established among men.

[1] Prov 8:15; Dan 2:21; Jn 19:11; Rom 13:1. [2] Ex 18:20. [3] Deut 1:16; Deut 16:19; Judg 21:25; Ps 82; Jer 21:12; Jer 22:3; 1 Pet 2:13, 14. [4] Ps 2; Rom 13:4a; 1 Tim 2:1–4. [5] Mt 17:27; Mt 22:21; Rom 13:7; Tit 3:1; 1 Pet 2:17. [6] Acts 4:19; Acts 5:29. [7] 2 Pet 2:10; Jude 8.

Article 37: Of the Last Judgment, Resurrection of the Body, and Eternal Life

Finally, we believe, according to the Word of God, that when the time, ordained by the Lord but unknown to all creatures, has come[1] and the number of the elect is complete,[2] our Lord Jesus Christ will come from heaven, bodily and visibly,[3] as He ascended (Acts 1:11), with great glory and majesty.[4] He will declare Himself Judge of the living and the dead[5] and set this old

have free course; the kingdom of Jesus Christ may make progress; and every anti-Christian power may be resisted."

world afire in order to purge it.[6] Then all people—men, women, and children, who ever lived, from the beginning of the world to the end—will appear in person before this great Judge.[7] They will be summoned with the archangel's call and with the sound of the trumpet of God (1 Thess 4:16).

Those who will have died before that time will arise out of the earth,[8] as their spirits are once again united with their own bodies in which they lived. Those who will then be still alive will not die as the others but will be changed in the twinkling of an eye from perishable to imperishable.[9] Then the books will be opened and the dead will be judged (Rev 20:12) according to what they have done in this world, whether good or evil (2 Cor 5:10).[10] Indeed, all people will render account for every careless word they utter (Mt 12:36), which the world regards as mere jest and amusement. The secrets and hypocrisies of men will then be publicly uncovered in the sight of all. And so, for good reason, the thought of this judgment is horrible and dreadful to the wicked and evildoers[11] but it is a great joy and comfort to the righteous and elect. For then their full redemption will be completed and they will receive the fruits of their labor and of the trouble they have suffered.[12] Their innocence will be known to all and they will see the terrible vengeance that God will bring upon the wicked who persecuted, oppressed, and tormented them in this world.[13]

The wicked will be convicted by the testimony of their own consciences and will become immortal, but only to be tormented in the eternal fire[14] prepared for the devil and his angels (Mt 25:41).[15] On the other hand, the faithful and elect will be crowned with glory and honor. The Son of God will acknowledge their names before God His Father (Mt 10:32) and His elect angels.[16] God will wipe away every tear from their eyes (Rev

21:4),[17] and their cause—at present condemned as heretical and evil by many judges and civil authorities—will be recognized as the cause of the Son of God. As a gracious reward, the Lord will cause them to possess such a glory as the heart of man could never conceive.[18] Therefore, we look forward to that great day with a great longing to enjoy to the full the promises of God in Jesus Christ our Lord. Amen. Come, Lord Jesus! (Rev 22:20).

[1] Mt 24:36; Mt 25:13; 1 Thess 5:1,2. [2] Heb 11:39, 40; Rev 6:11. [3] Rev 1:7. [4] Mt 24:30; Mt 25:31. [5] Mt 25:31–46; 2 Tim 4:1; 1 Pet 4:5. [6] 2 Pet 3:10–13. [7] Deut 7:9–11; Rev 20:12, 13. [8] Dan 12:2; Jn 5:28, 29. [9] 1 Cor 15:51, 52; Phil 3:20, 21. [10] Heb 9:27; Rev 22:12. [11] Mt 11:22; Mt 23:33; Rom 2:5, 6; Heb 10:27; 2 Pet 2:9; Jude 15; Rev 14:7a. [12] Lk 14:14; 2 Thess 1:3–10; 1 Jn 4:17. [13] Rev 15:4; Rev 18:20. [14] Mt 13:41, 42; Mk 9:48; Lk 16:22–28; Rev 21:8. [15] Rev 20:10. [16] Rev 3:5. [17] Is 25:8; Rev 7:17. [18] Dan 12:3; Mt 5:12; Mt 13:43; 1 Cor 2:9; Rev 21:9–22:5.

An Introduction to the Heidelberg Catechism

The Reformation in the Palatinate

The Palatinate, one of the finest provinces of Germany, on both sides of the upper Rhine, was one of the seven electorates (*Kurfürstenthümer*), whose rulers, in the name of the German people, elected the Emperor of Germany. After the dissolution of the old empire (1806) it ceased to be a politico-geographical name, and its territory is now divided between Baden, Bavaria, Hesse Darmstadt, Nassau, and Prussia. Its capital was Heidelberg (from 1231 till 1720), famous for its charming situation at the foot of the Königsstuhl (king's chair), on the banks of the Swabian River Neckar, for its picturesque castle and for its university (founded in 1346).

Luther made a short visit to Heidelberg in 1518 and defended certain evangelical theses. In 1546, the year of Luther's death, the Reformation was introduced under the Elector Frederick II. Melanchthon—who was a native of the Palatinate and twice received a call to a professorship of theology at Heidelberg (1546 and 1557), but declined—acted as the chief counselor in the work and aided, on a personal visit in 1557, in reorganizing the university on an evangelical basis under Otto Henry (1556–59).

He may therefore be called the Reformer of the Palatinate. He impressed upon it the character of a moderate Lutheranism friendly to Calvinism. The Augsburg Confession was adopted as the doctrinal basis and the cultus was remodeled (as also in the neighboring Duchy of Württemberg) after Zwinglian simplicity. Heidelberg now began to attract Protestant scholars from different countries and became a battle-ground of Lutheran, Philippist, Calvinist, and Zwinglian views. The conflict was enkindled as usual by the zeal for the real presence of Christ during the sacrament of communion. Tilemann Heshusius—whom Melanchthon without knowing his true character had recommended to a theological chair (1558)—introduced in his position as General Superintendent exclusive Lutheranism; he excommunicated Deacon Klebitz for holding the Zwinglian view and even fought with him at the altar about the communion cup. This public scandal was the immediate occasion of the Heidelberg Catechism.

Frederick III

During this controversy, Frederick III, surnamed the Pious (1515–1576), became Elector of the Palatinate in 1559. He made it the chief object of his reign to carry out the reformation begun by his predecessors. He tried at first to conciliate the parties and asked the advice of Melanchthon, who, a few months before his death, counseled peace, moderation, and biblical simplicity and warned against extreme and scholastic subtleties in the doctrine of the Lord's Supper.[1] Frederick III deposed both

[1] *Responsio Ph. Mel. ad quæstionem de controversia Heidelbergensi* (Nov. 1, 1559), in *Corp. Reform.* Vol. IX. pp. 960 sqq. It is the last public utterance of Melanchthon on the eucharistic question and agrees substantially with the doctrine of Calvin, as it was afterwards expressed in the Heidelberg Catechism.

Heshusius and Klebitz, arranged a public disputation (June 1560) on the eucharist, decided in favor of the Melanchthonian or Calvinistic view, called distinguished foreign divines to the university, and entrusted two of them with the composition of the Heidelberg Catechism, which was to secure harmony of teaching and to lay a solid foundation for the religious instruction of the rising generation.

Frederick was one of the purest and noblest characters among the princes of Germany. He was to the Palatinate what King Alfred and Edward VI were to England, what the Electors Frederick the Wise and John the Constant were to Saxony, and Duke Christopher to Württemberg. He did more for educational and charitable institutions than all his predecessors. He devoted to them the entire proceeds of the oppressed convents. He lived in great simplicity that he might contribute liberally from his private income to the cause of learning and religion. He was the first German prince who professed the Reformed Creed, as distinct from the Lutheran. For this he suffered much reproach and was threatened with exclusion from the benefits of the Augsburg Treaty of Peace (concluded in 1555), since Zwinglianism and Calvinism were not yet tolerated on German soil. But at the Diet of Augsburg, in 1566, he made before the Emperor a manly confession of his faith and declared himself ready to lose his crown rather than violate his conscience. Even his opponents could not but admire his courage, and the Lutheran Elector Augustus of Saxony applauded him, saying, "Fritz, thou art more pious than all of us." He praised God on his deathbed that he had been permitted to see such a reformation in Church and school that men were led away from human traditions to Christ and his divine Word. He left in writing a full confession of his faith, which may be regarded as an authentic explanation of the Heidelberg Catechism; it was published after his death by his son, John Casimir (1577).

Ursinus and Olevianus

Frederick showed his wisdom by calling two young divines, Ursinus and Olevianus, to Heidelberg to aid in the Reformation and to prepare an evangelical catechism. They belong to the reformers of the second generation. Theirs it was to nurture and to mature rather than to plant. Both were Germans, but well acquainted with the Reformed Churches in Switzerland and France. Both suffered deposition and exile for the Reformed faith.

Zacharias Ursinus (Bär), the chief author of the Heidelberg Catechism, was born at Breslau, July 18, 1534, and studied seven years (1550–1557) at Wittenberg under Melanchthon, who esteemed him as one of his best pupils and friends. He accompanied his teacher to the religious conference at Worms, 1557, and to Heidelberg, and then proceeded on a literary journey to Switzerland and France. He made the personal acquaintance of Bullinger and Peter Martyr at Zurich, of Calvin and Beza at Geneva, and was thoroughly initiated into the Reformed Creed. Calvin presented him with his works and wrote in them the best wishes for his young friend. On his return to Wittenberg, he received a call to the rectorship of the Elizabeth College at Breslau. After the death of Melanchthon, he went a second time to Zurich (October 1560), intending to remain there. In the following year, he was called to a theological chair at Heidelberg. Here he labored with untiring zeal and success till the death of Frederick III, 1576, when, together with six hundred steadfast Reformed ministers and teachers, he was deposed and exiled by Louis VI, who introduced the Lutheran Creed. Ursinus found a refuge at Neustadt an der Hardt, and established there, with other deposed professors, a flourishing theological school under the protection of John Casimir, the second son of Frederick III. He died in the prime of his life and usefulness, March 6, 1583, leaving a widow and one son. In the same year, Casimir succeeded his Lutheran brother in the Electorate, recalled the exiled preachers, and re-established the Reformed Church in the Palatinate.

Ursinus was a man of profound classical, philosophical, and theological learning, poetic taste, rare gift of teaching, and fervent piety. His devotion to Christ is beautifully reflected in the first question of the Heidelberg Catechism and in his saying that he would not take a thousand worlds for the blessed assurance of being owned by Jesus Christ. He was no orator and no man of action, but a retired, modest, and industrious student.[2] His principal works, besides the Catechism, are a Commentary on the Catechism (*Corpus doctrinæ orthodoxæ*) and a defense of the Reformed Creed against the attacks of the Lutheran Formula of Concord.

* * *

Caspar Olevianus (Olewig), born at Treves on August 10, 1536, studied the ancient languages at Paris, Bourges, and Orleans and studied theology at Geneva and Zurich. He enjoyed, like Ursinus, the personal instruction and friendship of the surviving reformers of Switzerland. He began to preach the evangelical doctrines at

[2] On the door of his study, he inscribed the warning, "*Amice, quisquis huc venis, aut agita paucis, aut abi, aut me laborantem adjuva.*"

Treves, was thrown into prison, but soon released and called to Heidelberg in 1560 by Frederick III, who felt under personal obligation to him for saving one of his sons from drowning at the risk of his own life. He taught theology and preached at the court. He was the chief counselor of the Elector in all affairs of the Church. In 1576 he was banished on account of his faith and accepted a call to Herborn, 1584, where he died, February 27, 1585. His last word was a triumphant "*certissimus*,' in reply to a friend who asked him whether he was certain of his salvation. Theodore Beza lamented his death in a Latin poem, beginning

Eheu, quibus suspiriis,
Eheu, quibus te lacrymis
Oleviane, planxero?

Olevianus was inferior to Ursinus in learning, but his superior in the pulpit and in church government. He wrote an important catechetical work on the covenant of grace and is regarded as the forerunner of the federal theology of Coccejus and Lampe. He labored earnestly, but only with moderate success, for the introduction of the Presbyterian form of government and a strict discipline after the model of Geneva. Thomas Erastus (Lieber), Professor of Medicine at Heidelberg and afterwards of Ethics at Basle (died 1583), opposed excommunication and defended the supremacy of the state in matters of religion; hence the term "Erastianism" (equivalent to Cæsaropapism).

Preparation and Publication of the Catechism

The Heidelberg Catechism, as it is called after the city of its birth, or the Palatinate (also Palatine) Catechism, as it is named after the country for which it was intended, was prepared on the basis of two Latin drafts of Ursinus and a German draft of Olevianus. The peculiar gifts of both, the didactic clearness and precision of the one, and the pathetic warmth and unction of the other, were blended in beautiful harmony and produced a joint work which is far superior to all the separate productions of either. In the Catechism, they surpassed themselves. They were in a measure inspired for it. At the same time, they made free and independent use of the Catechisms of Calvin, Lasky, and Bullinger. The Elector took the liveliest interest in the preparation and even made some corrections.

In December, 1562, Frederick submitted the work to a general synod of the chief ministers and teachers assembled at Heidelberg, for revision and approval. It was published early in 1563, in German, under the title *Catechismus, Or Christian Instruction, as conducted in the Churches and Schools of the Electoral Palatinate.* It is preceded by a short Preface of the Elector, dated Tuesday, January 19, 1563, in which he informs the superintendents, clergymen, and schoolmasters of the Palatinate that, with the counsel and co-operation of the theological faculty and leading ministers of the Church, he had caused to be made and set forth a summary instruction or Catechism of our Christian religion from the Word of God, to be used hereafter in churches and schools for the benefit of the rising generation.

The Third Edition and the Eightieth Question

There appeared, in the year 1563, three official editions of the Catechism with an important variation in the eightieth question, which denounces the Romish mass as "a denial of the one sacrifice of Christ, and as an accursed idolatry." In the first edition, this question was wanting altogether; the second edition has it in part; the third in full, as it now stands.[3] This question was inserted by the express command of the Elector, perhaps by his own hand, as a Protestant counter-blast to the Romish anathemas of the Council of Trent, which closed its sessions on December 4, 1563. Hence the remark at the end of the second and third editions:

> What has been overlooked in the first print, as especially on folio 55 [which contains the eightieth question], has now been added by command of his electoral grace. 1563.

The same view of the Romish doctrine of transubstantiation and the sacrifice of the mass was generally entertained by the Reformers and is set forth as strongly in the Articles of Smalcald and other symbolical books, both Lutheran and Reformed. It must be allowed to remain as a solemn protest against idolatry. But the wisdom of inserting controversial matter into a catechism for the instruction of the youth has been justly doubted. The eightieth question disturbs the peaceful harmony of the book; it rewards evil for evil; it countenances intolerance, which is un-Protestant and unevangelical. It provoked much unnecessary hostility and led even, under the Romish rule of the Elector Charles Philip, in 1719, to the prohibition of the Catechism; but the loud remonstrance of England, Prussia, Holland, and other Protestant states forced the Elector to withdraw the tyrannical decree within a year, under certain conditions, to save appearances.

[3] By the discovery of the copy of the first ed., 1864, the origin of the eightieth question was satisfactorily decided. A second copy of the original ed. is in the Imperial Library of Vienna. The Brit. Museum contains a copy of the Engl. trans. by "William Turner, Doctor of Physick, Imprinted at London, by Richard Jones, 1572."—ED.

Translations

The Heidelberg Catechism was translated into all the European and many Asiatic languages. It has the pentecostal gift of tongues in a rare degree. It is stated that, next to the Bible, the *Imitation of Christ* by Thomas à Kempis, and Bunyan's *Pilgrim's Progress,* no book has been more frequently translated, more widely circulated and used. Whole libraries of paraphrases, commentaries, sermons, attacks, and defenses were written about it. In many Reformed churches, especially in Holland (and also in the United States), it was, and is to some extent even now, obligatory or customary to explain the Catechism from the pulpit every Sunday afternoon. Hence, the division of the questions into fifty-two Sundays, in imitation of the example set by Calvin's Catechism.[4]

A Latin translation for the use of colleges was made by order of the Elector, by Joshua Lagus and Lambert Ludolph Pithopœus, and appeared soon after the German, since Olevianus sent a copy of each to Bullinger, in Zurich, as early as April, 1563.[5] It is, however, much inferior to the German in force and unction. The Latin text was often edited separately as well as in the works of Ursinus, in connection with his commentary and other Latin commentaries and in collections of Reformed symbols.[6]

[4] This division was first introduced in the Latin edition of 1566, perhaps earlier. Van Alpen, Niemeyer, and others are wrong in dating it from the German edition of 1573 or 1575.

[5] Dœdes gives a facsimile of the title-page of the Latin edition of 1563, from a copy in the University Library at Utrecht. It is nearly the same as the title of the edition of 1566.

[6] Niemeyer (pp. 428 sqq.) reproduces the edition of 1584, which agrees with the *ed. princeps* of 1563 (as far as I can judge from the few fac-simile pages given by Dœdes), and with the text in the Oxford *Sylloge,* while that in the Græco-Latin edition of Sylburg slightly differs. Dr. Louis H. Steiner, of Frederick City, Md., published an elegant and accurate edition under the title "*Catechesis Religionis Christianæ seu Catechismus Heidelbergensis*. Baltimore, 1862." He gives the variations of three Latin editions: of Cambridge, 1585; of Geneva, 1609 (formerly in the possession of Chevalier Bunsen); and the Oxford *Sylloge*, 1804.

There are three Dutch translations: the first appeared at Emden, 1563; the second, by Peter Dathenus, in connection with a Dutch version of the Psalter, in 1566, and very often separately.[7]

A Greek translation was prepared by a distinguished classical scholar, D. Frid. Sylburg, 1597.[8]

Besides these there are editions in modern Greek, in Hebrew, Arabic, etc.[9]

Three or four English translations were made from the Latin, and obtained a wide circulation in Scotland, England, and America.[10] A more correct one from the German original was prepared for the tercentenary celebration of the Catechism, by a learned

[7] On the Dutch translations, see especially the learned work of Professor Dœdes, of Utrecht, pp. 74–128, with facsimiles at the end of the volume.

[8] I have before me a Græco-Latin edition of the Catechism κατηχήσεις τῆς χριστανικῆς θρησκείας, by Sylburg, and of the Belgic Confession by Jac. Revius, printed at Utrecht, 1660. Earlier editions I see noticed in catalogues.

[9] Niemeyer (*Proleg.* p. lxii.) mentions a Polish translation by *Prasmovius*, a Hungarian by *Scarasius*, an Arabic by *Chelius*, a Singalese by *Konyer*, besides French, Italian, Spanish, English, Bohemian, modern Greek, and Hebrew versions. Dœdes (p. 41) adds a Persian and a Malayan translation. There is no doubt many other versions.

[10] An English edition, without the name of the translator, appeared A.D. 1591 at Edinburgh, "by publick Authority, for the Use of Scotland," and also repeatedly in connection with the "Psalm-Book and the Book of Common Order." It is embodied in Dunlop's *Collection of Confessions of Faith*, etc., *of publick authority in the Church of Scotland* (Edinburgh, 1719–1722), Vol. II. pp. 273–361, and reproduced by Dr. Horatius Bonar in his *Catechisms of the Scottish Reformation* (London, 1866), pp. 112–170. Dr. Bonar says (p. 171): "There are several translations of the Heidelberg or Palatine Catechism; and our Church [the Church of Scotland] seems not to have kept to one. In the edition of the Book of Common Order before us (1615), the Catechism is given alone; in that which Dunlop has followed, it has the 'Arguments' and 'Uses' of Bastingius." Another translation by Bishop Henry Parry, of Worcester (d. 1616), appeared (together with the commentary of Ursinus) at Oxford, 1509 and 1601. It was often republished—at Edinburgh, 1615 (with sundry variations, see Bonar, p. 172), again in London, 1633, 1645, 1728, 1851, and quite recently (from the Oxford edition of 1601, with the variations of the edition of 1728) by Dr. Gerhart and Dr. Louis Steiner in the "Mercersburg Review" for 1861, pp. 74 sqq. The one now in use in the Dutch and German Reformed Churches in America, is traced (by the late Dr. De Witt of New York) to Dr. Laidlie, originally from Scotland, minister at Flushing, Long Island, and was adopted, 1771, by the Synod of the Reformed Dutch Church. These three English translations seem to be only different recensions of one translation compared with the Latin text.

and able committee appointed by the German Reformed Synod in Pennsylvania, but has not yet come into public use.[11]

The merits of the Latin and English translations and their relation to the German original may be seen from the following specimens:

The German Original, 1563	The Latin Version, 1563
FRAGE 1. Was ist dein einiger Trost im Leben und im Sterben? Das ich mit Leib und Seele, beides im Leben und im Sterben, nicht mein, sondern meines getreuen Heilandes Jesu Christi eigen bin, der mit seinem theuren Blute für alle meine Sünden vollkommen bezahlet, und mich aus aller Gewalt des Teufels erlöset hat; und also bewahret, dass ohne den Willen meines Vaters im Himmel kein Haar von meinem Haupte kann fallen, ja auch mir alles zu meiner Seligkeit dienen muss. Darum er mich auch durch seinen heiligen Geist des ewigen Lebens versichert, und ihm forthin zu leben von Herzen willig und bereit macht. FRAGE 2. Wie viele Stücke sind dir nöthig zu wissen, dass du in diesem Troste seliglich leben und sterben mögest?	QU. 1. *Quæ est unica tua consolatio in vita et in morte?* Quod animo pariter et corpore, sive vivam, sive moriar, non meus, sed fidissimi Domini et Servatoris mei Jesus Christi sum proprius, qui pretioso sanguine suo pro omnibus peccatis meis plenissime satisfaciens, me ab omni potestate diaboli liberavit, meque ita conservat, ut sine voluntate patris mei cœlestis, ne pilus quidem de meo capite posit cadere: imò verò etiam omnia saluti meæ servire oporteat. Quocirca me quoque suo Spiritu de vita æterna certum facit, utque ipsi deinceps vivam promptum ac paratum reddit. QU. 2. *Quot sunt tibi scitu necessaria, ut ista consolatione fruens, beatè vivas et moriaris?*

[11] See the tercentenary triglot edition of 1863.

Drei Stücke: Erstlich, wie gross meine Sünde und Elend sei. Zum Andern, wie ich von allen meinen Sünden und Elend erlöset werde. Und zum Dritten, wie ich Gott für solche Erlösung soll dankbar sein.	Tria. Primum, quanta sit peccati mei et miseriæ meæ magnitudo. Secundum, quo pacto ab omni peccato et miseria liberer. Tertium, quam gratiam Deo pro ea liberatione debeam.

Scotch Edition of 1591 *from Dunlop's Collection* (1722)	**Bishop Perry's Translation (1591)** *Oxford Edition of* 1601
Ques. 1. *What is thy only comfort in life and in death?* That in soul and body, whether I live or die, I am not mine own, but I belong unto my most faithful Lord and Saviour, Jesus Christ: who by his precious blood, most fully satisfying for all my sins, hath delivered me from the whole power of the Devil; and doth so preserve me, that without the will of my heavenly Father, not so much as a hair can fall from my head: yea, all things are made to serve for my salvation. Wherefore by his Spirit also, he assureth me of everlasting life, and maketh me ready and prepared, that henceforth I may live unto him.	*Ques.* 1. *What is thy only comfort in life and death?* That both in soul and body, whether I live or die, I am not mine own, but belong wholly unto my most faithful Lord and Saviour Jesus Christ, who by his precious blood most fully satisfying for all my sins, hath delivered me from all the power of the devil, and so preserveth me, that without the will of my heavenly Father not so much as a hair may fall from my head, yea all things must serve for my safety. Wherefore by his Spirit also he assureth me of everlasting life, and maketh me ready, and prepared, that henceforth I may live to him.

Ques. 2. *How many things are needful for thee to know, to the end [that] thou, enjoying this comfort, mayest live and die an happy man?* Three things. First, What is the greatness of my sin, and of my misery. Secondly, By what means I may be delivered from all my sin and misery. Thirdly, What thankfulness I owe to God for that deliverance.	Ques. 2. *How many things are necessary for thee to know, that thou enjoying this comfort mayest live and die happily?* Three. The first, what is the greatness of my sin and misery. The second, how I am delivered from all sin and misery. The third, what thanks I owe unto God for this delivery.

The Received American Version, 1771	**The New American Version, 1863**
Ques. 1. *What is thy only comfort in life and death?* That I with body and soul, both in life and death, am not my own, but belong unto my faithful Saviour Jesus Christ, who, with his precious blood, hath fully satisfied for all my sins, and delivered me from all the power of the devil; and so preserves me that without the will of my heavenly Father, not a hair can fall from my head; yea, that all things must be subservient to my salvation; and therefore, by his Holy Spirit, he also assures me of eternal life, and makes me sincerely willing and	Ques. 1. *What is thy only comfort in life and in death?* That I, with body and soul, both in life and in death, am not my own, but belong to my faithful Saviour Jesus Christ, who with His precious blood has fully satisfied for all my sins, and redeemed me from all the power of the devil; and so preserves me, that without the will of my Father in heaven not a hair can fall from my head; yea, that all things must work together for my salvation. Wherefore, by His Holy Spirit, He also assures me of eternal life, and makes me heartily willing and

ready henceforth, to live unto him.	ready henceforth to live unto Him.
Ques. 2. How many things are necessary for thee to know, that thou, enjoying this comfort, mayest live and die happily?	*Ques. 2. How many things are necessary for thee to know, that thou in this comfort mayest live and die happily?*
Three; the first, how great my sins and miseries are; the second, how I may be delivered from all my sins and miseries; the third, how I shall express my gratitude to God for such deliverance.	Three things: First, the greatness of my sin and misery. Second, how I am redeemed from all my sins and misery. Third, how I am to be thankful to God for such redemption.

NOTE: All the English versions, except the last, follow the Latin in its departures from the German, as "*most* faithful Lord" (*fidelissimi Domini*) for "faithful" (*getreuen*), "heavenly Father" (*Patris cœlestis*) for "Father in heaven" (*Vater im Himmel*). The dependence on the Latin may be seen also in the words "most fully satisfying" (*plenissime satisfaciens*), "delivered" (*liberavit*) for "redeemed" (*erlöset*), "delivery" (*liberatio*) for "redemption" (*Erlösung*) and in the omission of "heartily" (*von Herzen*), for which, however, the common American version (which seems to have made use also of the Dutch version) substitutes "sincerely."

Character and Aim

The Heidelberg Catechism answers the double purpose of a guide for the religious instruction of the youth and a confession of faith for the Church.

As a catechism, it is an acknowledged masterpiece, with few to equal, and none to surpass it. Its only defect is that its answers are mostly too long for the capacity and memory of children. It is intended for a riper age. Hence, an abridgment was made as early as 1585, but no attempts to simplify and popularize it have been able to supersede it.

As a standard of public doctrine, the Heidelberg Catechism is the most catholic and popular of all the Reformed symbols. The German Reformed Church acknowledges no other. The Calvinistic system is herein set forth with wise moderation, and without its sharp, angular points. This may be a defect in logic, but it is an advantage in religion, which is broader and deeper than logic. Children and the mass of the people are unable to appreciate metaphysical distinctions and the transcendent mysteries of eternal decrees. The doctrine of election to holiness and salvation in Christ (or the positive and edifying part of the dogma of predestination) is indeed incidentally set forth as a source of humility, gratitude, and comfort (Questions 1, 31, 53, 54), but nothing is said of a *double* predestination, or of an eternal decree of *reprobation,* or of a *limited* atonement (comp. Question 37). These difficult questions are left to private opinion and theological science. This reserve is the more remarkable since the authors (as well as all other Reformers, except Melanchthon in his later period) were strict predestinarians.

Plan and Arrangement

The Heidelberg Catechism follows the order of the Epistle to the Romans and is divided into three parts. The first two questions are introductory. The first part treats of the sin and misery of man (Questions 3–11; comp. Rom. 1:18—3:20); the second of the redemption by Christ (Questions 12–85; comp. Rom. 3:21—11:36); the third of the thankfulness of the redeemed, or the Christian life (Questions 86–129; comp. Rom. 12–16). The second part is the largest and contains an explanation of all the articles of the Apostles' Creed under the three heads of God the Father, God the Son, and God the Holy Ghost. The doctrine of the sacraments is rightly incorporated in this part, instead of being treated in separate sections, as in the Roman and Lutheran Catechisms. The third part gives an exposition of the Decalogue (as a rule of obedience, viewed in the light of redemption) and of the Lord's Prayer.

This order corresponds to the development of religious life and to the three leading ideas of repentance, faith, and love. The conception of Christian life, as an expression of gratitude for redeeming grace, is truly evangelical. In older catechisms, the five or six parts of a catechism—namely, the Creed, the Decalogue, the Lord's Prayer, Baptism, the Lord's Supper—are mechanically coordinated; here they are worked up into an organic system.

The execution is admirable throughout. Several answers are acknowledged gems in the history of catechetical literature—e.g., the definition of faith (Ques. 21), on providence (Ques. 27 and 28), on the significance of the Christian name (Ques. 31 and 32), on the benefit of the ascension (Ques. 49), and on justification by faith (Ques. 60).

The Spirit of the Catechism

The genius of the Catechism is brought out at once in the first question, which contains the central idea and strikes the keynote. It is unsurpassed for depth, comfort, and beauty, and, once committed to memory, can never be forgotten. It represents

Christianity in its evangelical, practical, cheering aspect, not as a commanding law, not as an intellectual scheme, not as a system of outward observances, but as the best gift of God to man, as a source of peace and comfort in life and in death. What can be more comforting, what at the same time more honoring and stimulating to a holy life than the assurance of being owned wholly by Christ our blessed Lord and Saviour, who sacrificed his own spotless life for us on the cross? The first question and answer of the Heidelberg Catechism is the whole gospel in a nutshell; blessed is he who can repeat it from the heart and hold it fast to the end.[12]

It would be difficult to find a more evangelical definition of faith than in Question 21:

> Faith is not only a certain knowledge, whereby I hold for truth all that God has revealed to us in his Word; but also a hearty trust, which the Holy Spirit works in me by the gospel, that not only to others, but to me also, forgiveness of sins, everlasting righteousness, and salvation are freely given by God, merely of grace, only for the sake of Christ's merits.

How rich and consoling is the lesson derived from God's all-ruling Providence in Question 28!

[12] Dr. Nevan (*Tercentenary Edition*, Introd. p. 95) says: "No question in the whole Catechism has been more admired than this, and none surely is more worthy of admiration. Where shall we find, in the same compass, a more beautifully graphic, or a more impressively full and pregnant representation of all that is comprehended for us in the grace of our Lord and Saviour Jesus Christ? For thousands and tens of thousands, during the past three hundred years, it has been as a whole system of theology in the best sense of the term, their pole-star over the sea of life, and the sheet-anchor of their hope amid the waves of death. But what we quote it for now is simply to show the mind that actuates and rules the Catechism throughout. We have here at once its fundamental conception and the reigning law of its construction; the key-note, we may say, which governs its universal sense, and whose grandly solemn tones continue to make themselves heard through all its utterances from beginning to end."

> That we may be patient in adversity, thankful in prosperity, and for what is future have good confidence in our faithful God and Father, that no creature shall separate us from his love, since all creatures are so in his hand that without his will they cannot so much as move.

The Catechism is a work of religious enthusiasm, based on solid theological learning, and directed by excellent judgment. It is baptized with the pentecostal fire of the great Reformation, yet remarkably free from the polemic zeal and intolerance which characterized that wonderfully excited period—by far the richest and deepest in Church history next to the age of Christ and his inspired apostles. It is the product of the heart as well as the head, full of faith and unction from above. It is fresh, lively, glowing, yet clear, sober, self-sustained. The ideas are biblical and orthodox, and well-fortified by apt Scripture proofs.[13] The language is dignified, terse, nervous, popular, and often truly eloquent. It is the language of devotion as well as instruction. Altogether, the Heidelberg Catechism is more than a book: It is an institution and will live as long as the Reformed Church.

Comparisons with the Lutheran and Westminster Catechisms

The Heidelberg Catechism stands mediating between Luther's Small Catechism, which appeared thirty-four years earlier

[13] Ques. 44 is hardly an exception; for the idea therein expressed is no error *per se*, but only a false interpretation of the article on Christ's descent into hell (Hades) in the Apostles' Creed, which places it, as an actual fact, between death and the resurrection, in accordance with the Scriptures (Luke 23:43; Acts 2:27, 31; 1 Pet. 3:19; 4:6; Eph. 4:9, 10); while the Catechism, following Calvin and Lasky, understands it figuratively of Christ's suffering on the cross.

(1529), and the Westminster Shorter Catechism, which was prepared eighty-four years later (1647).

These are the three most popular and useful catechisms that Protestantism has produced and have still the strongest hold upon the churches they represent. They have the twofold character of catechisms and symbolical books. They are alike evangelical in spirit and aim; they lead directly to Christ as the one and all-sufficient Saviour and to the Word of God as the only infallible rule of the Christian's faith and life.

Luther's Catechism is the most churchly of the three and adheres to the Catholic tradition in its order and arrangement. It assigns a very prominent place to the Sacraments, treating them in separate chapters, coordinate with the Decalogue, the Creed, and the Lord's Prayer; while the others incorporate them in the general exposition of the articles of faith. Luther teaches baptismal regeneration and the corporeal presence, and even retains private confession and absolution as a quasi-sacrament. Heidelberg and Westminster are free from all remnants of sacerdotalism and sacramentalism and teach the Calvinistic theory of the sacraments, which rises, however, much higher than the Zwinglian.

On the other hand, the Lutheran and the Heidelberg Catechisms differ from the Westminster Catechism in the following points: (1) They retain the Apostles' Creed as the basis of doctrinal exposition, whereas the Westminster Catechism puts it in an appendix and substitutes a new logical scheme of doctrine for the old historical order of the Creed. (2) They are subjective and address the catechumen as a Church member, who answers from his real or prospective personal experience; while the Westminster Catechism is objective and impersonal and states the answer in an abstract proposition. (3) They use the warm and direct language of life, the Westminster the scholastic language of dogma; hence, the former two are less definite, but more expansive and suggestive than the Presbyterian formulary, which, on the other hand, far surpasses them in brevity, terseness, and accuracy of definition.

Upon the whole, we prefer the catechetical style and method of the creative Reformation period, because it is more biblical and fresh to that of the seventeenth century—the age of scholastic orthodoxy—although we freely concede the relative progress and peculiar excellences of the Westminster standard.[14]

The Heidelberg Catechism differs from that of Luther: (1) By its fullness and thoroughness, and hence it is better adapted to a maturer age; while that of Luther has the advantage of brevity and childlike simplicity, and adaptation to early youth. The one has one hundred and twenty-nine, the other only forty questions and answers, and of these only three are devoted to the exposition of the Apostles' Creed, while the Sacraments receive disproportionate attention.

(2) The Heidelberg Catechism gives the words of the Decalogue in full, according to the twentieth chapter of Exodus and follows the old Jewish and Greek division, which is adopted by

[14] "It may be questioned," says Dr. Bonar, of the Free Church of Scotland, "whether the Church gained anything by the exchange of the Reformation standards for those of the seventeenth century. The scholastic mold in which the latter are cast has somewhat trenched upon the ease and breadth which mark the former; and the skillful metaphysics employed at Westminster in giving lawyer-like precision to each statement have imparted a local and temporary aspect to the new which did not belong to the more ancient standards. Or, enlarging the remark, we may say that there is something about the theology of the Reformation which renders it less likely to become obsolete than the theology of the covenant. The simpler formulas of the older age are quite as explicit as those of the later; while by the adoption of the Biblical in preference to the scholastic mode of expression they have secured for themselves a buoyancy which will bear them up when the others go down. The old age of that generation is likely to be greener than that of their posterity" (*Catechisms of the Scottish Reformation*, Preface, p. viii.).

the best commentators; while Luther presents merely an abridgment[15] and follows the Roman division by omitting the second commandment and splitting the tenth into two.

(3) The former gives a summary of the law, through which comes the knowledge of sin, in the first part (Ques. 3 and 4), but explains the Decalogue in the third division, viewing it in its Christian aspect as a permanent rule of life; while Luther regards the law in its Jewish or pedagogic aspect, as a schoolmaster leading men to Christ, and hence he puts it as the first head before the Creed. Ursinus correctly says: "The Decalogue belongs to the first part so far as it is a mirror of our sin and misery, but also to the third part as being the rule of our new obedience and Christian life."[16]

(4) In the rendering of the Creed, besides minor verbal differences, the Heidelberg Catechism retains "the holy catholic Church," with the addition of "Christian" (*eine heilige allgemeine christliche Kirche*); while Luther's omits "catholic," and substitutes for it "Christian."[17]

(5) In the Lord's Prayer, the Heidelberg Catechism uses the modern form "Our Father" (*Unser Vater*), while Luther in his Catechism (though not in his translation of Matt. 6:9 and Luke 11:2) adheres to the Latin and old German form of 'Father our' (*Vater unser*), a difference tenaciously maintained by German Lutherans. The former divides the Prayer into six petitions (with

[15] For example, the fourth (third) commandment is thus condensed: "*Du sollst den Feiertag heiligen*" (Thou shalt keep holy the rest-day).

[16] The Germans express the different aspects of the law by calling it a *Sündenspiegel, Sündenriegel,* and *Lebensregel,* a mirror of sin, a bar of sin, and a rule of life.

[17] Hence in Germany the term "Catholic" and "Romanist" are used synonymously, and the proverb "*Das ist um katholisch zu werden*" expresses a desperate condition of things. The English Churches have properly retained the term "catholic" in its good old sense, instead of allowing Romanists to monopolize it.

the Greek commentators), and renders ἐκ πονηροῦ "from the evil one" (*vom Bösen*, i.e., from the devil); while Luther (with Augustine) numbers seven petitions, and translates (herein agreeing with the English version) "from evil" (*vom Uebel*).

The difference between the Heidelberg and Westminster Catechisms is chiefly one of nationality. Where the choice is between the two, the former will be used in preference by Germans, the other by Scotch and English Presbyterians. The Westminster Shorter Catechism has the advantage of greater condensation and precision. It is not impossible to make a better one than either by blending the excellences of both. They represent also two types of piety: the one is more emotional and hearty, the other more scholastic and intellectual. This appears at once in the first question. The Heidelberg Catechism asks: "What is thy only *comfort* in life and in death?" The Westminster: "What is the chief *end* of man?" The one goes at once into the heart of evangelical piety—the mystical union of the believer with Christ; the other goes back to the creation and the glory of God; but both teach the same God and Christ, and the same way of salvation, whereby God is glorified, and man is raised to everlasting felicity in his enjoyment.

History of the Catechism

The Heidelberg Catechism was greeted with great joy and was at once introduced into the churches and schools of the Lower Palatinate; while the Upper Palatinate, under the governorship of Louis (the eldest son of Frederick III) remained strictly Lutheran.

But, like every good book, it had to pass through a trial of probation and a fire of martyrdom. Even before it was printed, an anonymous writer attacked the Heidelberg Synod which, in December, 1562, had adopted the Catechism in manuscript, together with sundry measures of reform.[18] After its publication, it was violently assailed by strict Lutherans for its alleged Zwinglian and Calvinistic heresies and by Jesuits on account of the condemnation of the idolatry of the mass in the eightieth question. The first opponents were Lutheran princes (Margrave Charles II of Baden, Duke Christopher of Württemberg, the Palatine of Zweibrücken), and Lutheran divines, such as Heshusius, Flacius, Brentius, and Andreæ.[19] Ursinus wrote an able apology of his Catechism, which is embodied in several older editions since 1584. A theological colloquy was held at Maulbronn in April, 1564, where the theological leaders of the Lutheran Duchy of Württemberg and the Reformed Palatinate, in the presence of their princes, debated for six days in vain on the eucharist and the ubiquity of Christ's body. Both parties were confirmed in their opinions, though the Reformed had the best of the argument.

Frederick III, notwithstanding his appeal to Melanchthon and the altered Augsburg Confession, was openly charged with apostasy from the Lutheran faith and seriously threatened with exclusion from the peace of the empire. Even the liberal Emperor Maximilian II wrote him a letter of remonstrance. His fate was to be decided at the Diet of Augsburg, 1566. At this critical juncture,

[18] This curious document, which throws light upon that Synod hitherto little known, has been recently recovered and published by Wolters in the *Studien mud Kritiken* for 1867, No. 1, pp. 15 sqq. The Lutheran author, perhaps a dissenting member of the Synod, gives a list of the measures for the introduction of the Catechism and the abolition of various abuses, and accompanies them with bitter marginal comments, such as: "This is a lie and against God's Word"; "This is the Anabaptist heresy"; "To spread Zwinglianism"; "*Friss Vogel oder stirb*"; "*Ad spargendam zizaniam*"; "*Ut citius imbibant venenum*"; "*Evangelii abrogatio*"; "*Hispanica inquisitio.*"

[19] See on this Lutheran opposition Wolters, l.c., and in his earlier book, *Der Heidelb. Katechismus in seiner Urgestalt* (1864), pp. 141–196; Nevin, Introd. to the *Tercent. Ed.* pp. 42 sqq.; and especially Sudhoff, *Olevianus und Ursinus*, pp. 140 sqq.

the pious Elector boldly defended his Catechism, which, he said, was all taken from the Bible and so well fortified with marginal proof-texts that it could not be overthrown. He declared himself willing to yield to God's truth, if any one could show him anything better from the Scripture, which was at hand for the purpose. Altogether he made, at the risk of his crown and his life, such a noble and heroic confession as reminds us of Luther's stand at the Diet of Worms. Even his Lutheran opponents were filled with admiration and praise and left him thereafter in quiet possession of his faith. "Why do ye persecute this man?" said the Margrave of Baden; "he has more piety than the whole of us." The Elector Augustus of Saxony gave similar testimony on this memorable occasion.[20]

Thus, the Catechism had gained a sort of legal existence in the German empire, although it was not till after the Thirty-Years' War, in the Treaty of Westphalia, that the Reformed Church, as distinct from the Lutheran, was formally recognized in Germany. After the death of Frederick, it had to pass through another persecution in the home of its birth. His successor, Louis VI (1576–1583), exiled its authors, and replaced it by Luther's Catechism and the Formula of Concord. But under the regency of Frederick's second son, Prince John Casimir, the Heidelberg Catechism and the Reformed Church were restored to their former honor, and continued to flourish till the outbreak of the Thirty-Years' War.

[20] Hundeshagen says of Frederick III: "He is acknowledged to be the greatest ruler which the evangelical Palatinate ever had, and as to personal piety and loyalty to his faith the shining model of an evangelical prince." See his art. on the City and University of Heidelberg, in the *Gedenkbuch der* 300 *jähr. Jubelfeier des Heidelb. Kat.* pp. 58, 59.

This war brought terrible devastation and untold misery upon Heidelberg and the Palatinate, which were laid waste by the merciless Tilly (1622). Then followed the repeated invasions of Turenne, Melac, and Marshal de Lorges, under Louis XIV. The Palatinate fell even into the hands of Roman Catholic rulers (1685) and never again rose to its former glory. Thousands of Protestants emigrated to America and planted the Catechism in Pennsylvania so that what it lost in the old world it gained in the new. The indifferentism and rationalism of the eighteenth century allowed all creeds to go into disuse and neglect. In the nineteenth century, faith revived and with it respect for the Heidelberg Catechism; but, owing to the introduction of the union of the Lutheran and Reformed Churches in the Grand Duchy of Baden, to which Heidelberg now belongs, it was merged into a new catechism compiled from it and from that of Luther.[21]

* * *

The history of the Palatinate Catechism extends far beyond the land of its birth. It took deeper root and acquired greater influence in other countries. Soon after its appearance, it commended itself by its intrinsic excellences to all Reformed Churches of the German tongue. It was introduced in East Friesland, Jülich (Juliers), Cleve (Cleves), Berg, the Wupperthal, Bremen, Hesse Cassel, Anhalt, Brandenburg, East and West Prussia, the free imperial cities, in Hungary, Poland, and in several cantons of Switzerland,

[21] On the symbolical status of the Evangelical Church in Baden, see two essays of Dr. Hundeshagen, *Die Bekenntnissgrundlage der vereinigten evangelischen Kirche im Grossherzogthum Baden* (1851), and an address delivered before a Pastoral Conference at Durlach, on the same subject, 1851, republished in his *Schriften und Abhandlungen*, ed. by Dr. Christlieb, Gotha, 1875, Vol. II. pp. 119 sqq.

as St. Gall, Schaffhausen, and Berne.[22] In the royal house of Prussia it is still used in the instruction of the princes, even after the introduction of the union of the two confessions.[23]

It was surrounded with a large number of learned works which fill an important place in the history of Reformed theology. Eminent professors made it the basis of lectures in the University.

In no country was the Catechism more honored than in Holland and her distant colonies in Asia and Africa. It soon replaced the catechisms of Calvin and Lasky. The synods of Wesel, 1568, of Emden, 1571, and of Dort, 1574, recommended and enjoined its use; and ministers were required to explain it to the people in fifty-two lessons throughout the year in the afternoon service of the Lord's Day.

In the beginning of the sixteenth century, the Arminians called for a revision of it to remove certain features to which they objected. But the famous General Synod of Dort, after a careful examination, opposed any change, and, in its 148th Session, May 1, 1619, it unanimously delivered the judgment that the Heidelberg Catechism

> formed altogether a most accurate compend of the orthodox Christian faith; being, with singular skill, not only adapted to the understanding of the young, but suited also for the advantageous instruction of older persons; so that it could continue to be taught with great edification

[22] The editions used in the Canton Berne have an anti-supralapsarian addition to Question 27: "*Und obwohl die Sünden durch Gottes Fürsehung werden regiert, so ist doch Gott keine Ursache der Sünde; denn das Ziel unterscheidet die Werke. Siehe Exempel an Joseph und seinen Brüdern, an David und Simei, an Christo und den Juden.*" This addition is found as early as 1697. Noticed by Trechsel in *Studien und Kritiken* for 1867, p. 574.

[23] So I [Philip Schaff] was informed by the late court chaplain, Dr. Snethlage, of Berlin, who was originally Reformed, and who confirmed several members of the royal family.

> in the Belgic churches, and ought by all means to be retained.

This judgment was agreed to by all the foreign delegates from Germany, Switzerland, and England, and has thus an œcumenical significance for the Reformed communion.

The Heidelberg Catechism was also clothed with symbolical authority in Scotland, and was repeatedly printed "by public authority," even after the Westminster standards had come into use. It seems to have there practically superseded Calvin's Catechism, but it was in turn superseded by Craig's Catechism, and Craig's by that of the Westminster Assembly.

* * *

From Holland the Heidelberg Catechism crossed the Atlantic to Manhattan Island (1609), with the discoverer of the Hudson River, and was the first Protestant catechism planted on American soil. A hundred years later, German emigrants, driven from the Palatinate by Romish persecution and tyranny, carried it to Pennsylvania and other colonies. It has remained ever since the honored symbol of the Dutch and German Reformed Churches in America and will continue to be used as long as they retain their separate denominational existence, or even if they should unite with the larger Presbyterian body.

One of the first acts of the reunited Presbyterian Church in the United States, at the session of the General Assembly in Philadelphia, May, 1870, was the formal sanction of the use of the Heidelberg Catechism in any congregation which may desire it.[24]

* * *

In the year 1863, three centuries after its first publication, the Heidelberg Catechism witnessed its greatest triumph, not only in Germany and Holland, but still more in a land which the authors never saw, and in a language the sound of which they probably never heard. The Reformation was similarly honored in 1817, and the Augsburg Confession in 1830, but no other catechism.

In Germany the tercentenary celebration of the Heidelberg Catechism was left to individual pastors and congregations, and called forth some valuable publications.[25]

The German Reformed Church in the United States took it up as a body and gave it a wider scope. She made the three-hundredth anniversary of her confession the occasion for a general revival of theological and religious life, the publication of a triglot

[24] A special committee, appointed by the Old School Assembly of 1869, reported to the first reunited Assembly of 1870, after a laudatory description of the Heidelberg Catechism, the following resolutions, which were unanimously adopted: 1. *Resolved,* That this General Assembly recognizes in the Heidelberg Catechism a valuable Scriptural compendium of Christian doctrine and duty. 2. *Resolved,* That if any churches desire to employ the Heidelberg Catechism in the instruction of their children, they may do so with the approbation of this Assembly. See the *Minutes of the General Assembly of the Presbyterian Church in the United States of America for* 1870, p. 120, and the Memorial volume on *Presbyterian Reunion* (New York, 1870), p. 454.

[25] Among these we mention the articles on the Heidelberg Catechism by Ullmann, Sack, Plitt, Hundeshagen, Wolters, and Trechsel, in the *Studien und Kritiken* for 1863, 1864, and 1867, the discovery and reprint of the *ed. princeps* by Wolters (1864), and a collection of excellent sermons by distinguished Reformed pulpit orators, under the title, "*Der einzige Trost im Leben und Sterben,*" Elberfeld, 1863.

edition of the Catechism, the endowment of a tercentenary professorship in her seminary, and the collection of large sums of money for churches, missions, and other benevolent objects. All these ends were accomplished. The celebration culminated in a general convention of ministers and laymen in Philadelphia, which lasted a whole week, January 17–23, 1863, in the midst of the raging storm of the American Civil War. About twenty interesting and instructive essays on the Catechism and connected topics, which had been specially prepared for the occasion by eminent German, Dutch, and American divines, were read in two churches before crowded and attentive assemblies. Luther, Calvin, Zwingli, Melanchthon, Frederick III, Ursinus, and Olevianus were called from their graves to reproduce before an American audience the ideas, trials, and triumphs of the creative and heroic age of the Reformation. Altogether, the year 1863 marks an epoch in the history of the Heidelberg Catechism and of the German Reformed Church in America.[26]

[26] See the *Tercentenary Monument* (574 pages), and the *Gedenkbuch der dreihundert jährigen Jubelfeier des Heidelberger Katechismus* (449 pages), both published at Philadelphia. 1863. The German edition gives the correspondence and essays of Drs. Herzog, Ebrard, Ullmann, Hundeshagen, Lange, and Schotel, in the original German, together with a history of the Catechism by the editor. The Anglo-American essays and addresses of Drs. Nevin, Schaff, Gerhart, Harbaugh, Wolff, Bomberger, Porter, De Witt, Kieffer, Theodor and Thomas Appel, Schneck, Russell, Gans, and Bausmann, are found in full in the English edition.

The Heidelberg Catechism[1]
(1563)

Question 1. What is thy only comfort in life and death?

That I, with body and soul, both in life and death,[a] am not my own,[b] but belong unto my faithful Savior, Jesus Christ;[c] who, with His precious blood, has fully satisfied for all my sins,[d] and delivered me from all the power of the devil;[e] and so preserves me[f] that without the will of my heavenly Father, not a hair can fall from my head;[g] yea, that all things must be subservient to my salvation,[h] and therefore, by His Holy Spirit, He also assures me of eternal life,[i] and makes me sincerely willing and ready, henceforth, to live unto Him.[j]

[a] Rom.14:7, 8. [b] 1 Cor. 6:19. [c] 1 Cor. 3:23; Tit. 2:14. [d] 1 Pet. 1:18, 19; 1 John 1:7; 1 John 2:2, 12. [e] Heb. 2:14; 1 John 3:8; John 8:34–36. [f] John 6:39; John 10:28; 2 Thess. 3:3; 1 Pet. 1:5. [g] Matt. 10:29–31; Luke 21:18. [h] Rom. 8:28. [i] 2 Cor. 1:20–22; 2 Cor. 5:5; Eph. 1:13, 14; Rom. 8:16. [j] Rom. 8:14; 1 John 3:3.

Q. 2. How many things are necessary for thee to know that thou, enjoying this comfort, may live and die happily?

[1] Questions and answers are taken primarily from the 1863 edition.

Three:[a] the first, how great my sins and miseries are;[b] the second, how I may be delivered from all my sins and miseries;[c] the third, how I shall express my gratitude to God for such deliverance.[d]

[a] Matt. 11:28–30; Luke 24:46–48; 1 Cor. 6:11; Tit. 3:3–7. [b] John 9:41; John 15:22. [c] John 17:3; Acts 4:12; Acts 10:43. [d] Eph. 5:8–11; 1 Pet. 2:9, 10; Rom. 6:1, 2, 12, 13.

The First Part: Of The Misery Of Man

Q. 3. From whence knowest thou thy sins and misery?

Out of the law of God.[a]

[a] Rom.3:20.

Q. 4. What does the law of God require of us?

Christ teaches us in sum, Matthew 22:37–40, "Thou shalt love the Lord thy God with all thy heart, with all thy soul, and with all thy mind, and with all thy strength. This is the first and the great commandment; and the second is like unto it, Thou shalt love thy neighbour as thyself. On these two commandments hang all the law and the prophets."[a]

[a] Deut.6:5; Lev. 19:18; Mark 12:30; Luke 10:27.

Q. 5. Canst thou keep all these things perfectly?

No:[a] for I am prone by nature to hate God and my neighbor.[b]

[a] Rom. 3:10, 20, 23; 1 John 1:8,10. [b] Rom.8:7; Eph. 2:3; Tit. 3:3; Gen. 6:5; Gen. 8:21; Jer. 17:9; Rom. 7:23.

Q. 6. Did God then create man so wicked and perverse?

By no means; but God created man good,[a] and after His own image,[b] in true righteousness and holiness, that he might rightly know God his Creator, heartily love Him and live with Him in eternal blessedness, to praise and glorify Him.[c]

[a] Gen. 1:31. [b] Gen. 1:26, 27. [c] Col. 3:9, 10; Eph. 4:23, 24; 2 Cor. 3:18.

Q. 7. Whence then comes this depravity nature of mankind?

From the fall and disobedience of our first parents, Adam and Eve, in Paradise;[a] hence, our nature is become so corrupt that we are all conceived and born in sin.[b]

[a] Gen. 3; Rom. 5:12, 18, 19. [b] Ps. 51:5; Gen. 5:3.

Q. 8. Are we then so corrupt that we are wholly incapable of doing any good and inclined to all wickedness?

Indeed we are;[a] except we are regenerated by the Spirit of God.[b]

[a] Gen. 8:21; John 3:6; Gen. 6:5; Job 14:4; Job 15:14, 16, 36; Isa. 53:6. [b] John 3:3, 5; 1 Cor. 12:3; 2 Cor. 3:5.

Q. 9. Does not God then do injustice to man by requiring from him in His law that which he cannot perform?

Not at all;[a] for God made man capable of performing it; but man, by the instigation of the devil,[b] and his own willfull disobedience,[c] deprived himself and all his posterity of those divine gifts.

[a] Eph. 4:24; Eccl. 7:29. [b] John 8:44; 2 Cor. 11:3; Gen. 3:4. [c] Gen. 3:6; Rom. 5:12; Gen. 3:13; 1 Tim. 2:13, 14.

Q. 10. Will God suffer such disobedience and rebellion to go unpunished?

By no means; but is terribly displeased[a] with our original as well as actual sins; and will punish them in His just judgment temporally and eternally,[b] as He has declared, "Cursed is every one that continueth not in all things, which are written in the book of the law, to do them."[c]

[a] Gen. 2:17; Rom. 5:12. [b] Ps. 5:5; Ps. 50:21; Nah. 1:2; Exod. 20:5; Exod. 34:7; Rom. 1:18; Eph. 5:6; Heb. 9:27. [c] Deut. 27:26; Gal. 3:10.

Q. 11. Is not God then also merciful?

God is indeed merciful,[a] but also just;[b] therefore, His justice requires that sin, which is committed against the most high majesty of God, be also punished with extreme, that is, with everlasting punishment of body and soul.

[a] Exod. 34:6, 7; Exod. 20:6. [b] Ps. 7:9; Exod. 20:5; Exod. 23:7; Exod. 34:7; Ps. 5:5, 6; Nah. 1:2, 3.

The Second Part: Of Man's Deliverance

Q. 12. Since then, by the righteous judgment of God, we deserve temporal and eternal punishment, is there no way by which we may escape that punishment and be again received into favor?

God will have His justice satisfied:[a] and therefore we must make this full satisfaction, either by ourselves or by another.[b]

[a] Gen. 2:17; Exod. 20:5; Exod. 23:7; Ezek. 18:4; Matt. 5:26; 2 Thess. 1:6; Luke 16:2. [b] Rom. 8:3, 4.

Q. 13. Can we ourselves then make this satisfaction?

By no means; but on the contrary, we daily increase our debt.[a]

[a] Job 9:2, 3; Job 15:15, 16; Job 4:18, 19; Ps. 130:3; Matt. 6:12; Matt. 18:25; Matt. 16:26.

Q. 14. Can there be found anywhere, one, who is a mere creature, able to satisfy for us?

None; for, first, God will not punish any other creature for the sin which man has committed;[a] and further, no mere creature can sustain the burden of God's eternal wrath against sin, so as to deliver others from it.[b]

[a] Ezek. 18:4; Gen. 3:17; Heb. 2:14–17. [b] Nah. 1:6; Ps. 130:3.

Q. 15. What sort of a mediator and deliverer then must we seek?

One who is very man and perfectly[a] righteous;[b] and yet more powerful than all creatures; that is, one who is also very God.[c]

[a] 1 Cor. 15:21; Jer. 33:16; Isa. 53:9; 2 Cor. 5:21. [b] Heb. 7:16, 26. [c] Isa. 7:14; Isa. 9:6; Rom. 9:5; Jer. 23:5, 6; Jer. 23:6; Luke 11:22.

Q. 16. Why must he be a true and sinless man?

Because the justice of God requires that the same human nature which has sinned should likewise make satisfaction for sin;[a] and one, who is himself a sinner, cannot satisfy for others.[b]

[a] Ezek. 18:4, 20; Rom. 5:12, 15, 18; 1 Cor. 15:21; Heb. 2:14–16; 1 Pet. 3:18; Isa. 53:3–5, 10, 11. [b] Heb. 7:26, 27; Ps. 49:7, 8; 1 Pet. 3:18.

Q. 17. Why must he be at the same time true God?

That he might, by the power of his Godhead,[a] sustain in his human nature,[b] the burden of God's wrath;[c] and might obtain for and restore to us righteousness and life.[d]

[a] Isa. 9:6; Isa. 63:3. [b] Isa. 53:4, 11. [c] Deut. 4:24; Nah. 1:6; Ps. 130:3. [d] Isa. 53:5, 11; Acts 2:24; 1 Pet. 3:18; John 3:16; Acts 20:28; John 1:4.

Q. 18. Who, then, is that Mediator who is at the same time true God and a true, sinless man?

Our Lord Jesus Christ,[a] who is freely given unto us for complete redemption and righteousness.[b]

[a] 1 Tim. 2:5; Heb. 2:9; Matt. 1:23; 1 Tim. 3:16; Luke 2:11. [b] 1 Cor. 1:30.

Q. 19. Whence knowest thou this?

From the holy gospel: which God Himself first revealed in Paradise;[a] afterwards published by the holy Patriarchs[b] and Prophets,[c] and foreshadowed by the sacrifices and other ceremonies of the law;[d] and finally, fulfilled by His only-begotten Son.[e]

[a] Gen. 3:15. [b] Gen. 22:18; Gen. 12:3; Gen. 49:10, 11. [c] Isa. 53; Isa. 42:1–4; Isa. 43:25; Isa. 49:5, 6, 22, 23; Jer. 23:5, 6; Jer. 31:32, 33; Jer. 32:39–41; Mic. 7:18–20; Acts 10:43; Rom. 1:2; Heb. 1:1; Acts 3:22–24; Acts 10:43; John 5:46. [d] Heb. 10:1, 7; Col. 2:7; John 5:46. [e] Rom. 10:4; Gal. 4:4, 5; Gal. 3:24; Col. 2:17.

Q. 20. Are all men then saved by Christ, as they have perished by Adam?

No;[a] only such as by true faith are ingrafted into Him and receive all His benefits.[b]

[a] Matt.7:14; Matt.22:14. [b] Mark 16:16; John 1:12; John 3:16, 18, 36; Isa. 53:11; Ps. 2:12; Rom. 11:17, 19, 20; Rom. 3:22; Heb. 4:2, 3; Heb. 5:9; Heb. 10:39; Heb. 11:6.

Q. 21. What is true faith?

True faith is not only a certain knowledge, whereby I hold for truth all that God has revealed to us in His word,[a] but also an assured confidence,[b] which the Holy Ghost[c] works by the gospel in my heart;[d] that not only to others, but to me also, forgiveness of sins, everlasting righteousness and salvation,[e] are freely given by God, merely of grace, only for the sake of Christ's merits.[f]

[a] Jas. 2:19. [b] 2 Cor. 4:13; Eph. 2:7–9; Eph. 3:12; Gal. 2:16; Heb. 11:1, 7–10; Heb. 4:16; Jas. 1:6; Matt. 16:17; Philip. 1:19; Rom. 4:16–21; Rom. 5:1; Rom. 1:16; Rom. 10:10, 17; Rom. 3:24, 25. [c] Gal. 5:22; Matt. 16:17; 2 Cor. 4:13; John 6:29; Eph. 2:8; Philip. 1:19; Acts 16:14. [d] Rom. 1:16; Rom. 10:17; 1 Cor. 1:21; Acts 10:44; Acts 16:14. [e] Rom. 1:17; Gal. 3:11; Heb. 10:10, 38; Gal. 2:16. [f] Eph. 2:8; Rom. 3:24; Rom. 5:19; Luke 1:77, 78.

Q. 22. What is it then necessary for a Christian to believe?

All things promised us in the gospel,[a] which the articles of our catholic, undoubted Christian faith teach us in sum.

[a] John 20:31; Matt. 28:19; Mark 1:15.

Q. 23. What are these Articles?

I believe in God the Father, Almighty, Maker of heaven and earth:

And in Jesus Christ, His only begotten Son, our Lord: who was conceived by the Holy Ghost, born of the Virgin Mary; suffered under Pontius Pilate, was crucified, dead, and buried; He descended into hades; the third day He rose from the dead; He ascended into heaven and sitteth at the right hand of God the Father Almighty; from thence He shall come to judge the quick and the dead.

I believe in the Holy Ghost: the Holy Catholic Church; the communion of saints; the forgiveness of sins; the resurrection of the body, and the life everlasting.

Q. 24. How are these Articles divided?

Into three parts: The first is of God the Father and our creation; the second, of God the Son and our redemption; the third, of God the Holy Ghost and our sanctification.

Q. 25. Since there is but one Divine Being,[a] why speakest thou of three: Father, Son, and Holy Ghost?

Because God has so revealed Himself in His word,[b] that these three distinct Persons are the one, true, eternal God.

[a] Deut. 6:4; Eph. 4:6; Isa. 44:6; Isa. 45:5; 1 Cor. 8:4, 6. [b] Isa. 61:1; Luke 4:18; Gen. 1:2, 3; Ps. 33:6; Isa. 48:16; Ps. 110:1; Matt. 3:16, 17; Matt. 28:19; 1 John 5:7; Isa. 6:1, 3; John 14:26; John 15:26; 2 Cor. 13:13; Gal. 4:6; Eph. 2:18; Tit. 3:5, 6.

Of God the Father

Q. 26. What believest thou when thou sayest, "I believe in God the Father Almighty, Maker of heaven and earth"?

That the eternal Father of our Lord Jesus Christ (who of nothing made heaven and earth, with all that is in them;[a] who likewise upholds and governs the same by His eternal counsel and providence)[b] is for the sake of Christ, His Son, my God and my Father;[c] on whom I rely so entirely, that I have no doubt, but He will provide me with all things necessary for soul and body[d] and further, that He will make whatever evils He sends upon me, in this valley of tears turn out to my advantage;[e] for He is able to do it, being Almighty God,[f] and willing, being a faithful Father.[g]

[a] Gen. 1, 2; Job 33:4; Job 38, 39; Ps. 33:6; Acts 4:24; Acts 14:15; Isa. 45:7. [b] Matt. 10:29; Heb. 1:3; Ps. 104:27–30; Ps. 115:3; Matt. 10:29; Eph. 1:11. [c] John 1:12; Rom. 8:15; Gal. 4:5–7; Eph. 1:5. [d] Ps. 55:23; Matt. 6:25, 26; Luke 12:22. [e] Rom. 8:28. [f] Rom.10:12; Luke 12:22; Rom. 8:23; Isa. 46:4; Rom. 10:12. [g] Matt. 6:25–34; Matt. 7:9–11.

Q. 27. What dost thou mean by the providence of God?

The almighty and everywhere present power of God;[a] whereby, as it were by His hand, He upholds and governs[b] heaven, earth, and all creatures; so that herbs and grass, rain and drought,[c] fruitful and barren years, meat and drink, health and sickness,[d] riches and poverty,[e] yea, and all things come, not by chance, but be His fatherly hand.[f]

[a] Acts 17:25–28; Jer. 23:23, 24; Isa. 29:15, 16; Ezek. 8:12. [b] Heb. 1:3. [c] Jer. 5:24; Acts 14:17. [d] John 9:3. [e] Prov. 22:2. [f] Matt. 10:20; Prov. 16:33.

Q. 28. What does it profit us to know that God has created, and by His providence does still upholds all things?

That we may be patient in adversity;[a] thankful in prosperity;[b] and that in all things, which may hereafter befall us, we place our firm trust in our faithful God and Father[c] that nothing shall separate us from His love;[d] since all creatures are so in his hand, that without His will they cannot so much as move.[e]

[a] Rom. 5:3; Jas. 1:3; Ps. 39:9; Job 1:21, 22. [b] Deut. 8:10; 1 Thess. 5:18. [c] Ps. 55:22; Rom. 5:4. [d] Rom. 8:38, 39. [e] Job 1:12; Job 2:6; Acts 17:25, 28; Prov. 21:1.

Of God the Son

Q. 29. Why is the Son of God called "Jesus," that is, Saviour?

Because He saves us and delivers us from our sins;[a] and no salvation is to be either sought or found in any other.[b]

[a] Matt. 1:21; Heb. 7:24,25. [b] Acts 4:12; John 15:4,5; 1 Tim. 2:5; Isa. 43:11; 1 John 5:11.

Q. 30. Do such then believe in the only Savior, Jesus, who seek their salvation and welfare of saints, of themselves, or anywhere else?

They do not; for though they boast of Him in words, yet in deeds they deny Jesus the only deliverer and Savior;[a] for one of these two things must be true: that either Jesus is not a complete Savior; or that they, who by a true faith receive this Savior, must find all things in Him necessary to their salvation.[b]

[a] 1 Cor. 1:13, 30, 31; Gal. 5:4. [b] Heb. 12:2; Isa. 9:6; Col. 1:19, 20; Col. 2:10; 1 John 1:7, 16.

Q. 31. Why is He called "Christ," that is, Anointed?

Because He is ordained of God the Father and anointed with the Holy Ghost,[a] to be our chief Prophet and Teacher,[b] who has fully revealed to us the secret counsel and will of God concerning our redemption;[c] and to be our only High Priest,[d] who by the one sacrifice of His body has redeemed us[e] and makes continual intercession with the Father for us;[f] and also to be our eternal King, who governs us by His word and Spirit and who defends and preserves us in that salvation He has purchased for us.[g]

[a] Heb. 1:9; Ps. 45:8; Isa. 61:1; Luke 4:18. [b] Deut. 18:15; Acts 3:22; Acts 7:37; Isa. 55:4. [c] John 1:18; John 15:15. [d] Ps. 110:4. [e] Heb. 10:12, 14; Heb. 9:12, 14, 28. [f] Rom. 8:34; Heb. 9:24; 1 John 2:1; Rom. 5:9, 10. [g] Ps. 2:6; Zech. 9:9; Matt. 21:5; Luke 1:33; Matt. 28:18; John 10:28; Rev. 12:10, 11.

Q. 32. But why art thou called a Christian?[a]

Because I am a member of Christ by faith[b] and thus am partaker of His anointing;[c] that so I may confess His name[d] and present myself a living sacrifice of thankfulness to Him:[e] and also that with a free and good conscience, I may fight against sin and Satan in this life [f] and afterwards I reign with Him eternally, over all creatures.[g]

[a] Acts 11:26. [b] 1 Cor. 6:15. [c] 1 John 2:27; Acts 2:17. [d] Matt. 10:32; Rom. 10:10; Mark 8:38. [e] Rom. 12:1; 1 Pet. 2:5, 9; Rev. 5:8, 10; Rev. 1:6. [f] 1 Pet. 2:11; Rom. 6:12, 13; Gal. 5:16, 17; Eph. 6:11; 1 Tim. 1:18, 19. [g] 2 Tim. 2:12; Matt. 25:34.

Q. 33. Why is Christ called God's "only begotten Son," since we are also the children of God?

Because Christ alone is the eternal and natural Son of God;[a] but we are children of God by adoption through grace for His sake.[b]

[a] John 1:1–3, 14, 18; Heb. 1:1, 2; John 3:16; 1 John 4:9; Rom. 8:32. [b] Rom. 8:15–17; John 1:12; Gal. 4:6; Eph. 1:5, 6.

Q. 34. Why callest thou Him "our Lord"?

Because He hath redeemed us, both soul and body, from all our sins, not with silver or gold, but with His precious blood and has delivered us from all the power of the devil; and thus has made us His own property.[a]

[a] 1 Pet. 1:18, 19; 1 Pet. 2:9; 1 Cor. 6:20; 1 Cor. 7:23; 1 Tim. 2:6; John 20:28.

Q. 35. What is the meaning of: "Conceived by the Holy Ghost, born of the Virgin Mary"?

That God's eternal Son, who is, and continues[a] true and eternal God,[b] took upon him the very nature of man, of the flesh and blood of the virgin Mary,[c] by the operation of the Holy Ghost;[d] that he might also be the true seed of David,[e] like unto his brethren in all things,[f] sin excepted.[g]

[a] Rom. 1:4; Rom. 9:5. [b] 1 John 5:20; John 1:1; John 17:3; Rom. 1:3; Col. 1:15. [c] Gal. 4:4; Luke 1:31, 42, 43. [d] John 1:14; Matt. 1:18, 20; Luke 1:32, 35. [e] Ps. 132:11; Rom. 1:3; 2 Sam. 7:12; Acts 2:30. [f] Philip. 2:7; Heb. 2:14, 17. [g] Heb. 4:15.

Q. 36. What profit dost thou receive from the holy conception and birth of Christ?

That He is our Mediator;[a] and with His innocence and perfect holiness, covers in the sight of God, my sins, wherein I was conceived and brought forth.[b]

[a] Heb. 7:26, 27; Heb. 2:17. [b] 1 Pet. 1:18, 19; 1 Pet. 3:18; 1 Cor. 1:30, 31; Rom. 8:3, 4; Isa. 53:11; Ps. 32:1.

Q. 37. What dost thou understand by the words "He suffered"?

That He, all the time that He lived on earth, but especially at the end of His life, sustained in body and soul, the wrath of God against the sin of the whole human race;[a] that so by his passion, as the only propitiatory sacrifice,[b] He might redeem our body and soul from everlasting damnation,[c] and obtain for us the favor of God, righteousness, and eternal life.[d]

[a] Isa. 53:4; 1 Pet. 2:24; 1 Pet. 3:18; 1 Tim. 2:6. [b] Isa. 53:10, 12; Eph. 5:2; 1 Cor. 5:7; 1 John 2:2; 1 John 4:10; Rom. 3:25; Heb. 9:28; Heb. 10:14. [c] Gal. 3:13; Col. 1:13; Heb. 9:12; 1 Pet. 1:18, 19. [d] Rom. 3:25; 2 Cor. 5:21; John 3:16; John 6:51; Heb. 9:15; Heb. 10:19.

Q. 38. Why did he suffer "under Pontius Pilate, as judge"?

That He, being innocent, and yet condemned by a temporal judge,[a] might thereby free us from the severe judgement of God to which we were exposed.[b]

[a] John 18:38; Matt. 27:24; Acts 4:27, 28; Luke 23:14, 15; John 19:4.[b] Ps. 69:4; Isa. 53:4, 5; 2 Cor. 5:21; Gal. 3:13.

Q. 39. Is there anything more in His having been "crucified," than if He had died some other death?

Yes there is; for thereby I am assured, that He took on Him the curse which lay upon me;[a] for the death of the cross was accursed of God.[b]

[a] Gal. 3:13. [b] Deut. 21:23.

Q. 40. Why was it necessary for Christ to humble Himself even "unto death"?

Because with respect to the justice and truth of God,[a] satisfaction for our sins could be made no otherwise than by the death of the Son of God.[b]

[a] Gen. 2:17. [b] Rom. 8:3, 4; Heb. 2:9, 14, 15.

Q. 41. Why was He "buried"?

To show thereby that He was really dead.[a]

[a] Matt. 27:59, 60; Luke 23:52, 53; John 19:38–42; Acts 13:29.

Q. 42. Since then Christ died for us, why must we also die?

Our death is not a satisfaction for our sins,[a] but only an abolishing of sin and a passage into eternal life.[b]

[a] Mark 8:37; Ps. 49:7. [b] John 5:24; Philip. 1:23; Rom. 7:24.

Q. 43. What further benefit do we receive from the sacrifice and death of Christ on the cross?

That by virtue thereof, our old man is crucified, dead, and buried with Him;[a] that so the corrupt inclinations of the flesh may no more reign in us;[b] but that we may offer ourselves unto Him a sacrifice of thanksgiving.[c]

[a] Rom. 6:6. [b] Rom. 6:6–8, 11, 12; Col. 2:12. [c] Rom. 12:1.

Q. 44. Why is it added, "He descended into hades"?

That in my greatest temptations, I may be assured, and wholly comfort myself in this, that my Lord Jesus Christ, by His inexpressible anguish, pains, terrors, and hellish agonies, in which He was plunged during all His sufferings,[a] but especially on the cross, has delivered me from the anguish and torments of hell.[b]

[a] Ps. 18:5, 6; Ps. 116:3; Matt. 26:38; Heb. 5:7; Isa. 53:10; Matt. 27:46. [b] Isa. 53:5.

Q. 45. What benefit do we receive from the "resurrection" of Christ?

First, by His resurrection, He has overcome death, that He might make us partakers of that righteousness which He had purchased for us by His death;[a] secondly, we are also by His power raised up to a new life;[b] and lastly, the resurrection of Christ is a sure pledge of our blessed resurrection.[c]

[a] 1 Cor. 15:16; Rom. 4:25; 1 Pet.1:3. [b] Rom. 6:4; Col.3:1, 3; Eph. 2:5, 6. [c] 1 Cor. 15:12, 20, 21; Rom. 8:11.

Q. 46. How dost thou understand the words: "He ascended into heaven"?

That Christ, in sight of His disciples, was taken up from earth into heaven;[a] and that He continues there for our interest,[b] until He comes again to judge the quick and the dead.[c]

[a] Acts 1:9; Matt. 26:64; Mark 16:19; Luke 24:51. [b] Heb. 7:25; Heb. 4:14; Heb. 9:24; Rom. 8:34; Eph. 4:10; Col. 3:1. [c] Acts 1:11; Matt. 24:30.

Q. 47. Is not Christ then with us even to the end of the world, as He has promised?[a]

Christ is very man and very God; with respect to His human nature, He is no more on earth;[b] but with respect to His Godhead, majesty, grace and spirit, He is at no time absent from us.[c]

[a] Matt. 28:20. [b] Heb. 8:4; Matt. 26:11; John 16:28; John 17:11; Acts 3:21. [c] John 14:17–19; John 16:13; Matt. 28:20; Eph. 4:8, 12.

Q. 48. But if His human nature is not present, wherever His Godhead is, are not then these two natures in Christ separated from one another?

By no means; for since the Godhead is incomprehensible and everywhere present,[a] it must necessarily follow that the same is beyond the limits of the human nature He assumed,[b] and yet is nevertheless in this human nature, and remains personally united to it.

[a] Acts 7:49; Jer. 23:24. [b] Col. 2:9; John 3:13; John 11:15; Matt. 28:6.

Q. 49. What benefit do we receive from Christ's ascension into heaven?

First, that He is our advocate in the presence of His Father in heaven;[a] secondly, that we have our flesh in heaven as a sure pledge that He, as the head, will also take up to Himself, us, His members;[b] thirdly, that He sends us His Spirit as an earnest,[c] by whose power we "seek the things which are above, where Christ sitteth on the right hand of God, and not things on earth."[d]

[a] 1 John 2:1; Rom. 8:34. [b] John 14:2; John 17:24; John 20:17; Eph. 2:6. [c] John 14:16, 7; Acts 2:1–4, 33; 2 Cor. 1:22; 2 Cor. 5:5. [d] Col. 3:1; Philip. 3:14.

Q. 50. Why is it added: "and sitteth at the right hand of God"?

Because Christ is ascended into heaven for this end, that He might appear as head of His church,[a] by whom the Father governs all things.[b]

[a] Eph.1:20, 21, 23; Col. 1:18. [b] Matt. 28:18; John 5:22.

Q. 51. What benefit do we receive from this glory of our Head, Christ?

First, that by His Holy Spirit, He pours out heavenly graces upon us, His members;[a] and then that by His power He defends and preserves us against all enemies.[b]

[a] Acts 2:33; Eph.4:8. [b] Ps. 2:9; Ps. 110:1, 2; John 10:28; Eph.4:8.

Q. 52. What comfort is it to thee that "Christ shall come again to judge the quick and the dead"?

That in all my sorrows and persecutions, with uplifted head I look for the very same person, who before offered Himself for my sake, to the tribunal of God, and has removed all curse from me, to come as judge from heaven:[a] who shall cast all His and my enemies into everlasting condemnation,[b] but shall translate me with all His chosen ones to Himself, into heavenly joys and glory.[c]

[a] Luke 21:28; Rom. 8:23; Philip. 3:20; Tit. 2:13; 1 Thess. 4:16. [b] 2 Thess. 1:6, 8–10; Matt. 25:41–43. [c] Matt. 25:34; 2 Thess. 1:7.

Of God the Holy Ghost

Q. 53. What dost thou believe concerning the Holy Ghost?

First, that He is true and co-eternal God with the Father and the Son;[a] secondly, that He is also given me,[b] to make me by a true faith, partaker of Christ and all His benefits,[c] that He may comfort me[d] and abide with me for ever.[e]

[a] 1 John 5:7; Gen. 1:2; Isa. 48:16; 1 Cor. 3:16; 1 Cor. 6:19; Acts 5:3, 4. [b] Gal. 4:6; Matt. 28:19, 20; 2 Cor. 1:21, 22; Eph. 1:13. [c] Gal. 3:14; 1 Pet. 1:2; 1 Cor. 6:17. [d] Acts 9:31; John 15:26. [e] John 14:16; 1 Pet. 4:14.

Q. 54. What believest thou concerning the "holy catholic church"?

That the Son of God,[a] from the beginning to the end of the world,[b] gathers, defends, and preserves[c] to Himself by His Spirit and word,[d] out of the whole human race,[e] a church chosen to everlasting life,[f] agreeing in true faith;[g] and that I am and forever shall remain,[h] a living member thereof.[i]

[a] Eph. 5:26; John 10:11; Acts 20:28; Eph. 4:11–13. [b] Ps. 71:17, 18; Isa. 59:21; 1 Cor. 11:26. [c] Matt. 16:18; John 10:28–30; Ps. 129:1–5. [d] Isa. 59:21; Rom. 1:16; Rom. 10:14–17; Eph. 5:26. [e] Gen. 26:4; Rev. 5:9. [f] Rom. 8:29, 30; Eph. 1:10–13. [g] Acts 2:46; Eph. 4:3–6. [h] Ps. 23:6; 1 Cor. 1:8, 9; John 10:28; 1 John 2:19; 1 Pet. 1:5. [i] 1 John 3:14, 19–21; 2 Cor. 13:5; Rom. 8:10.

Q. 55. What dost thou understand by "the communion of saints"?

First, that all and every one, who believes, being members of Christ, are in common, partakers of Him, and of all His riches and gifts;[a] secondly, that every one must know it to be his duty, readily and cheerfully to employ his gifts, for the advantage and salvation of other members.[b]

[a] 1 John 1:3; 1 Cor. 1:9; Rom. 8:32; 1 Cor. 12:12, 13; 1 Cor. 6:17. [b] 1 Cor. 12:21; 1 Cor. 13:1, 5; Philip. 2:4–8.

Q. 56. What believest thou concerning "the forgiveness of sins"?

That God, for the sake of Christ's satisfaction, will no more remember my sins, neither my corrupt nature, against which I have to struggle all my life long;[a] but will graciously impute to me the righteousness of Christ,[b] that I may never be condemned before the tribunal of God.[c]

[a] 1 John 2:2; 1 John 1:7; 2 Cor. 5:19, 21. [b] Jer. 31:34; Ps. 103:3, 4; Ps. 103:10, 12; Mic. 7:19, 23–25. [c] Rom. 8:1–4; John 3:18; John 5:24.

Q. 57. What comfort does the "resurrection of the body" afford thee?

That not only my soul after this life shall be immediately taken up to Christ, its head;[a] but also, that this, my body, being raised by the power of Christ, shall be reunited with my soul and made like unto the glorious body of Christ.[b]

[a] Luke 16:22; Luke 23:43; Philip. 1:21, 23. [b] 1 Cor. 15:53, 54; Job 19:25, 26; 1 John 3:2; Philip. 3:21.

Q. 58. What comfort takest thou from the article of "life everlasting"?

That since I now feel in my heart the beginning of eternal joy,[a] after this life, I shall inherit perfect salvation, which "eye has not seen, nor ear heard, neither has it entered into the heart of man" to conceive and that to praise God therein for ever.[b]

[a] 2 Cor. 5:2, 3. [b] 1 Cor. 2:9; John 17:3.

Q. 59. But what does it profit thee now that thou believest all this?

That I am righteous in Christ, before God, and an heir of eternal life.[a]

[a] Hab. 2:4; Rom. 1:17; John 3:36.

Q. 60. How art thou righteous before God?

Only by a true faith in Jesus Christ;[a] so that, though my conscience accuse me, that I have grossly transgressed all the commandments of God, and kept none of them,[b] and am still inclined to all evil;[c] notwithstanding, God, without any merit of mine,[d] but only of mere grace,[e] grants and imputes to me[f] the perfect satisfaction,[g] righteousness, and holiness of Christ;[h] even so, as if I never had had nor committed any sin: yea, as if I had fully accomplished all that obedience which Christ has accomplished for me;[i] inasmuch as I embrace such benefit with a believing heart.[j]

[a] Rom. 3:21–25, 28; Rom. 5:1, 2; Gal. 2:16; Eph. 2:8, 9; Philip. 3:9. [b] Rom. 3:9. [c] Rom. 7:23. [d] Tit. 3:5; Deut. 9:6; Ezek. 36:22. [e] Rom. 3:24; Eph. 2:8. [f] Rom. 4:4, 5; 2 Cor. 5:19. [g] 1 John 2:2. [h] 1 John 2:1. [i] 2 Cor. 5:21. [j] Rom. 3:22; John 3:18.

Q. 61. Why sayest thou, that thou art righteous only by faith?

Not that I am acceptable to God, on account of the worthiness of my faith; but because only the satisfaction, righteousness, and holiness of Christ is my righteousness before God;[a] and that I cannot receive and apply the same to myself any other way than by faith only.[b]

[a] 1 Cor. 1:30; 1 Cor. 2:2. [b] 1 John 5:10.

Q. 62. But why cannot our good works be the whole or part of our righteousness before God?

Because that the righteousness, which can be approved of before the tribunal of God, must be absolutely perfect[a] and in all respects conformable to the divine law; and also, that our best works in this life are all imperfect and defiled with sin.[b]

[a] Gal. 3:10; Deut. 27:26. [b] Isa. 64:6.

Q. 63. How is it that our good works merit nothing, while yet it is God's will to reward them in this life and that which is to come?

This reward comes not of merit, but of grace.[a]

[a] Luke 17:10.

Q. 64. But does not this doctrine make men careless and profane?

By no means: for it is impossible that those, who are implanted into Christ by a true faith, should not bring forth fruits of thankfulness.[a]

[a] Matt. 7:18; John 15:5.

Q. 65. Since then we are made partakers of Christ and all His benefits by faith only, whence comes this faith?

From the Holy Ghost,[a] who works faith in our hearts by the preaching of the gospel, and confirms it by the use of the sacraments.[b]

[a] Eph. 2:8, 9; Eph. 6:23; John 3:5; Philip. 1:29. [b] Matt. 28:19, 20; 1 Pet. 1:22, 23.

Q. 66. What are the sacraments?

The sacraments are holy visible signs and seals, appointed of God for this end, that by the use thereof, He may the more fully declare and seal to us the promise of the gospel: namely, that He grants us freely the remission of sin and life eternal for the sake of that one sacrifice of Christ, accomplished on the cross.[a]

[a] Gen. 17:11; Rom. 4:11; Deut. 30:6; Lev. 6:25; Heb. 9:7–9, 24; Ezek. 20:12; Isa. 6:6, 7; Isa. 54:9.

Q. 67. Are both word and sacraments, then, ordained and appointed for this end, that they may direct our faith to the sacrifice of Jesus Christ on the cross, as the only ground of our salvation?[a]

Yes, indeed: for the Holy Ghost teaches us in the gospel, and assures us by the sacraments, that the whole of our salvation depends upon that one sacrifice of Christ made for us on the cross.

[a] Rom. 6:3; Gal. 3:27.

Q. 68. How many sacraments has Christ instituted in the New Testament?

Two: Holy Baptism and the Holy Supper.

OF HOLY BAPTISM

Q. 69. How is it signified and sealed unto thee in Holy Baptism, that thou has part in the one sacrifice of Christ upon the cross?

Thus: That Christ appointed this external washing with water,[a] adding thereto this promise,[b] that I am as certainly washed by his blood and Spirit from all the pollution of my soul, that is, from all my sins,[c] as I am washed externally with water, by which the filthiness of the body is commonly washed away.

[a] Matt. 28:19. [b] Matt. 28:19; Acts 2:38; Matt. 3:11; Mark 16:16; John 1:33; Rom. 6:3, 4. [c] 1 Pet. 3:21; Mark 1:4; Luke 3:3

Q. 70. What is it to be washed with the blood and Spirit of Christ?

It is to receive of God the remission of sins, freely, for the sake of Christ's blood, which he shed for us by his sacrifice upon the cross;[a] and also to be renewed by the Holy Ghost, and sanctified to be members of Christ, that so we may more and more die unto sin, and lead holy and unblamable lives.[b]

[a] Heb. 12:24; 1 Pet. 1:2; Rev. 1:5; Rev. 7:14; Zech. 13:1; Ezek. 36:25. [b] John 1:33; John 3:5; 1 Cor. 6:11; 1 Cor. 12:13; Rom. 6:4; Col. 2:12.

Q. 71. Where has Christ promised us that we are as certainly washed with His blood and Spirit as with the water of Baptism?

In the institution of baptism, which is thus expressed: "Go ye, therefore, and teach all nations, baptizing them in the name of the Father, and of the Son, and of the Holy Ghost" (Matt. 28:19). And, "he that believeth, and is baptized, shall be saved; but he that believeth not, shall be damned" (Mark 16:16). This promise is also repeated where the Scripture calls baptism "the washing of regeneration" (Tit. 3:5) and the washing away of sins (Acts 22:16).

Q. 72. Is then the external Baptism with water the washing away of sin itself?

No;[a] for only the blood of Jesus Christ and the Holy Spirit cleanse us from all sin.[b]

[a] Matt. 3:11; 1 Pet. 3:21; Eph. 5:26, 27. [b] 1 John 1:7; 1 Cor. 6:11.

Q. 73. Why, then, doth the Holy Ghost call Baptism "the washing of regeneration" and "the washing away of sins"?

God speaks thus not without great cause, namely, not only thereby to teach us that as the filth of the body is purged away by water, so our sins are removed by the blood and Spirit of Jesus Christ;[a] but especially that by this divine pledge and sign He may assure us that we are spiritually cleansed from our sins as really, as we are externally washed with water.[b]

[a] Rev. 1:5; Rev. 7:14; 1 Cor. 6:11. [b] Mark 16:16; Gal. 3:27.

Q. 74. Are infants also to be baptized?

Yes: for since they, as well as the adult, are included in the covenant and church of God;[a] and since redemption from sin[b] by the blood of Christ, and the Holy Ghost, the author of faith, is promised to them no less than to the adult;[c] they must therefore by Baptism, as a sign of the covenant, be also admitted into the Christian church; and be distinguished from the children of unbelievers[d] as was done in the old covenant or testament by circumcision,[e] instead of which baptism is instituted[f] in the new covenant.

[a] Gen. 17:7. [b] Matt. 19:14. [c] Luke 1:15; Ps. 22:10; Isa. 44:1–3; Acts 2:39. [d] Acts 10:47. [e] Gen. 17:14. [f] Col. 2:11–13.

Of The Holy Supper Of the Lord

Q. 75. How is it signified and sealed unto thee in the Holy Supper that thou dost partake of the one sacrifice of Christ on the cross an all His benefits?

Thus: That Christ has commanded me and all believers, to eat of this broken bread and to drink of this cup in remembrance of Him, adding these promises:[a] first, that His body was offered and broken on the cross for me, and His blood shed for me, as certainly as I see with my eyes, the bread of the Lord broken for me, and the cup communicated to me; and further, that He feeds and nourishes my soul to everlasting life, with His crucified body and shed blood, as assuredly as I receive from the hands of the minister and taste with my mouth the bread and cup of the Lord, as certain signs of the body and blood of Christ.

[a] Matt. 26:26–28; Mark 14:22–24; Luke 22:19, 20; 1 Cor. 10:16, 17; 1 Cor. 11:23–25; 1 Cor. 12:13.

Q. 76. What is it to eat the crucified body and drink the shed blood of Christ?

It is not only to embrace with believing heart all the sufferings and death of Christ and thereby to obtain the pardon of sin and life eternal;[a] but also, besides that, to become more and more united to His sacred body,[b] by the Holy Ghost, who dwells both in Christ and in us; so that we, though Christ is in heaven[c] and we on earth, are notwithstanding "flesh of his flesh and bone of his bone"[d] and that we live and are governed forever by one spirit,[e] as members of the same body are by one soul.

[a] John 6:35, 40, 47–54. [b] John 6:55, 56. [c] Col. 3:1; Acts 3:21; 1 Cor. 11:26. [d] Eph. 3:16; Eph. 5:29, 30, 32; 1 Cor. 6:15, 17, 19; 1 John 3:24; 1 John 4:13; John 14:23. [e] John 6:56–58; John 15:1–6; Eph. 4:15, 16.

Q. 77. Where has Christ promised that He will as certainly feed and nourish believers with His body and blood, as they eat of this broken bread and drink of this cup?

In the institution of the supper, which is thus expressed:[a]

"The Lord Jesus, the same night in which he was betrayed, took bread, and when he had given thanks, he brake it, and said: Take, eat, this is my body, which is broken for you; this do in remembrance of me. After the same manner also he took the cup, when he had supped, saying: This cup is the New Testament in my blood; this do ye, as often as ye drink it, in remembrance of me.

For, as often as ye eat this bread, and drink this cup, ye do show the Lord's death till he come" (1 Cor. 11:23–26).

This promise is repeated by the holy apostle Paul, where he says, "The cup of blessing which we bless, is it not the communion of the blood of Christ? The bread which we break, is it not the communion of the body of Christ? For we being many are one bread, and one body: for we are all partakers of that one bread" (1 Cor. 10:16, 17).

[a] 1 Cor. 11:23–25; Matt. 26:26–28; Mark 14:22–24; Luke 22:19, 20; 1 Cor. 10:16, 17.

Q. 78. Do then the bread and wine become the very body and blood of Christ?

Not at all:[a] but as the water in baptism is not changed into the blood of Christ, neither is the washing away of sin itself, being only the sign and confirmation thereof appointed of God;[b] so the bread in the Lord's supper is not changed into the very body of Christ;[c] though agreeably to the nature and properties of sacraments,[d] it is called the body of Christ Jesus.

[a] Matt. 26:29. [b] Eph. 5:26; Tit. 3:5. [c] Mark 14:24; 1 Cor. 10:16, 17, 26–28. [d] Gen. 17:10, 11, 14, 19; Exod. 12:11, 13, 27, 43, 48; Exod. 13:9; 1 Pet. 3:21; 1 Cor. 10:1–4.

Q. 79. Why then doth Christ call the bread "His body," and the cup "His blood," or "the new covenant in His blood"; and Paul the "communion of body and blood of Christ"?

Christ speaks thus, not without great reason, namely, not only thereby to teach us, that as bread and wine support this temporal life, so His crucified body and shed blood are the true meat and drink, whereby our souls are fed to eternal life;[a] but more especially by these visible signs and pledges to assure us, that we are as really partakers of His true body and blood by the operation of the Holy Ghost as we receive by the mouths of our bodies these holy signs in remembrance of Him;[b] and that all His sufferings and obedience are as certainly ours, as if we had in our own persons suffered and made satisfaction for our sins to God.

[a] John 6:51, 55. [b] 1 Cor. 10:16, 17.

Q. 80. What difference is there between the Lord's Supper and the Roman Catholic Mass?

The Lord's Supper testifies to us that we have a full pardon of all sin by the only sacrifice of Jesus Christ, which He Himself has once accomplished on the cross;[a] and, that we by the Holy Ghost are ingrafted into Christ,[b] who, according to His human nature is now not on earth, but in heaven, at the right hand of God His Father,[c] and will there be worshipped by us.[d] But the Mass teaches, that the living and dead have not the pardon of sins through the sufferings of Christ, unless Christ is also daily offered for them by the priests; and further, that Christ is bodily under the form of bread and wine, and therefore is to be worshipped in them; so that the Mass, at bottom, is nothing else than a denial of the one sacrifice and sufferings of Jesus Christ, and an accursed idolatry.[e]

[a] Heb. 7:27; Heb. 9:12, 25–28; Heb. 10:10, 12–14; John 19:30; Matt. 26:28; Luke 22:19, 20. [b] 1 Cor. 6:17; 1 Cor. 10:16. [c] Heb. 1:3; Heb. 8:1, 2; John 20:17. [d] Matt. 6:20, 21; John 4:21–24; Luke 24:52; Acts 7:55, 56; Col. 3:1; Philip. 3:20, 21; 1 Thess. 1:10; Heb. 9:6–10. [e] Heb. 9:26; Heb. 10:12, 14, 19–31.

Q. 81. For whom is the Lord's Supper instituted?

For those who are truly sorrowful for their sins, and yet trust that these are forgiven them for the sake of Christ; and that their remaining infirmities are covered by His passion and death; and who also earnestly desire to have their faith more and more strengthened, and their lives more holy; but hypocrites, and such as turn not to God with sincere hearts, eat and drink judgment to themselves.[a]

[a] 1 Cor. 10:19–22; 1 Cor. 11:28, 29.

Q. 82. Are they then also to be admitted to this Supper, who show themselves to be, by their confession and life, unbelieving and ungodly?

No; for by this, the covenant of God would be profaned, and His wrath kindled against the whole congregation;[a] therefore, it is the duty of the Christian Church, according to the appointment of Christ and His apostles, to exclude such persons, by the keys of the kingdom of heaven, till they show amendment of life.

[a] 1 Cor. 11:20, 34; Isa. 1:11–15; Isa. 66:3; Jer. 7:21–23; Ps. 50:16.

Q. 83. What are the keys of the kingdom of heaven?

The preaching of the holy gospel and Christian discipline, or excommunication out of the Christian Church; by these two, the kingdom of heaven is opened to believers and shut against unbelievers.

Q. 84. How is the kingdom of heaven opened and shut by the preaching of the Holy Gospel?

In this way: when according to the command of Christ, it is declared and publicly testified to all and every believer, that, whenever they receive the promise of the Gospel by a true faith, all their sins are really forgiven them of God, for the sake of Christ's merits; and on the contrary, when it is declared and testified to all unbelievers, and such as do not sincerely repent, that they stand exposed to the wrath of God, and eternal condemnation, so long as they are unconverted:[a] according to which testimony of the Gospel, God will judge them, both in this, and in the life to come.

[a] Matt. 16:18, 19; Matt. 18:15–19; John 20:21–23.

Q. 85. How is the kingdom of heaven shut and opened by Christian discipline?

In this way: when according to the command of Christ, those, who under the name of Christians, maintain doctrines, or practices inconsistent therewith, and will not, after having been often brotherly admonished, renounce their errors and wicked course of life, are complained of to the Church, or to those, who are thereunto appointed by the Church; and if they despise their admonition, are by them forbidden the use of the sacraments; whereby they are excluded from the Christian Church, and by God Himself from the kingdom of Christ; and when they promise and show real amendment, are again received as members of Christ and His Church.[a]

[a] Matt. 18:15–18; 1 Cor. 5:2–5, 11; 2 Thess. 3:14, 15; 2 Cor. 2:6–8.

The Third Part: Of Thankfulness

Q. 86. Since then we are delivered from our misery, merely of grace, through Christ, without any merit of ours, why must we still do good works?

Because Christ, having redeemed and delivered us by His blood, also renews us by His Holy Spirit, after His own image; that so we may testify, by the whole of our conduct, our gratitude to God for His blessings,[a] and that He may be praised by us;[b] also, that every one may be assured in himself of his faith,[c] by the fruits thereof; and that, by our godly conversation, others may be gained to Christ.[d]

[a] Rom. 6:13; Rom. 12:1, 2; 1 Pet. 2:5, 9, 10; 1 Cor. 6:20. [b] Matt. 5:16; 1 Pet. 2:12; 1 Pet. 1:6, 7. [c] 2 Pet. 1:10; Matt. 7:17; Gal. 5:6, 22, 23. [d] 1 Pet. 3:1, 2; Rom. 14:19.

Q. 87. Cannot they then be saved, who, continuing in their wicked and ungrateful lives, are not converted to God?

By no means; for, as the Scripture saith, no unchaste person, idolater, adulterer, thief, covetous man, drunkard, slanderer, robber, or any such like, shall inherit the kingdom of God.[a]

[a] 1 Cor. 6:9, 10; Eph. 5:5, 6; 1 John 3:14.

Q. 88. In how many things does true repentance or conversion consist?

In two things: the mortification of the old and the quickening of the new man.[a]

[a] Rom. 6:1, 4–6; Eph. 4:22–24; Col. 3:5–10; 1 Cor. 5:7; 2 Cor. 7:10.

Q. 89. What is the mortification of the old man?

It is a sincere sorrow of heart, that we have provoked God by our sins; and more and more to hate and flee from them.[a]

[a] Rom. 8:13; Joel 2:13; Hos. 6:1.

Q. 90. What is the quickening of the new man?

It is a sincere joy of heart in God, through Christ,[a] and with love and delight to live according to the will of God in all good works.[b]

[a] Rom. 5:1; Rom. 14:17; Isa. 57:15. [b] Rom. 6:10, 11; Gal. 2:20.

Q. 91. But what are good works?

Only those which proceed from a true faith,[a] are performed according to the law of God,[b] and to his glory;[c] and not such as are founded on our imaginations, or the institutions of men.[d]

[a] Rom. 14:23. [b] Lev. 18:4; 1 Sam. 15:22; Eph. 2:10. [c] 1 Cor. 10:31. [d] Deut. 12:32; Ezek. 20:18, 19; Isa. 29:13; Matt. 15:7–9.

Q. 92. What is the law of God?

God spake all these words, saying:

First Commandment

I am the LORD thy God, which have brought thee out of the land of Egypt, out of the house of bondage. Thou shalt have no other gods before me.

Second Commandment:

Thou shalt not make unto thee any graven image, or any likeness of any thing that is in heaven above, or that is in the earth beneath, or that is in the water under the earth. Thou shalt not bow down thyself to them, nor serve them; for I the LORD thy God am a jealous God, visiting the iniquity of the fathers upon the children unto the third and fourth generation of them that hate me, and shewing mercy unto thousands of them that love me, and keep my commandments.

Third Commandment:

Thou shalt not take the name of the LORD thy God in vain; for the LORD will not hold him guiltless that taketh his name in vain.

Fourth Commandment:

Remember the sabbath day, to keep it holy. Six days shalt thou labour, and do all thy work; but the seventh day is the sabbath of the LORD thy God: in it thou shalt not do any work, thou, nor thy son, nor thy daughter, thy manservant, nor thy maidservant, nor thy cattle, nor thy stranger that is within thy gates. For in six days the LORD made heaven and earth, the sea, and all that in them is, and rested the seventh day: wherefore the LORD blessed the sabbath day, and hallowed it.

Fifth Commandment:

Honour thy father and thy mother: that thy days may be long upon the land which the LORD thy God giveth thee.

Sixth Commandment:

Thou shalt not kill.

Seventh Commandment:

Thou shalt not commit adultery.

Eighth Commandment:

Thou shalt not steal.

Ninth Commandment:

Thou shalt not bear false witness against thy neighbour.

Tenth Commandment:

Thou shalt not covet thy neighbour's house, thou shalt not covet thy neighbour's wife, nor his manservant, nor his maidservant, nor his ox, nor his ass, nor any thing that is thy neighbour's.

Q. 93. How are these commandments divided?

Into two tables;[a] the first of which teaches us how we must behave towards God; the second, what duties we owe to our neighbor.[b]

[a] Exod. 34:28; Deut. 4:13; Deut. 10:3, 4. [b] Matt. 22:37–40.

Q. 94. What does God require in the first commandment?

That I, as sincerely as I desire the salvation of my own soul, avoid and flee from all idolatry,[a] sorcery, soothsaying, superstition,[b] invocation of saints, or any other creatures;[c] and learn rightly to know the only true God;[d] trust in Him alone,[e] with humility[f] and patience submit to Him;[g] expect all good things from Him only;[h] love,[i] fear,[j] and glorify Him with my whole heart;[k] so that I renounce and forsake all creatures, rather than commit even the least thing contrary to His will.[l]

[a] 1 John 5:21; 1 Cor. 6:9, 10; 1 Cor. 10:7, 14. [b] Lev. 19:31; Deut. 18:9–12. [c] Matt. 4:10; Rev. 19:10; Rev. 22:8, 9. [d] John 17:3. [e] Jer. 17:5, 7. [f] 1 Pet. 5:5,6. [g] Heb. 10:36; Col. 1:11; Rom. 5:3, 4; 1 Cor. 10:10; Philip. 2:14. [h] Ps. 104:27–30; Isa. 45:7; Jas. 1:17. [i] Deut. 6:5; Matt. 22:37. [j] Deut. 6:2; Ps. 111:10; Prov. 1:7; Prov. 9:10; Matt. 10:28. [k] Matt. 4:10; Deut. 10:20, 21. [l] Matt. 5:29, 30; Matt. 10:37; Acts 5:29.

Q. 95. What is idolatry?

Idolatry is, instead of, or besides that one true God, who has manifested Himself in His word, to contrive, or have any other object, in which men place their trust.[a]

[a] Eph. 5:5; 1 Chron. 16:26; Philip. 3:19; Gal. 4:8; Eph. 2:12; 1 John 2:23; 2 John 1:9; John 5:23.

Q. 96. What does God require in the second commandment?

That we in no wise represent God by images,[a] nor worship Him in any other way than He has commanded in His word.[b]

[a] Deut. 4:15–19; Isa. 40:18–25; Rom. 1:23, 24; Acts 17:29. [b] 1 Sam. 15:23; Deut. 12:30–32; Matt. 15:9.

Q. 97. Are images then not at all to be made?

God neither can, nor may be represented by any means:[a] but as to creatures; though they may be represented, yet God forbids to make, or have any resemblance of them, either in order to worship them or to serve God by them.[b]

[a] Isa. 40:25. [b] Exod. 23:24, 25; Exod. 34:13, 14, 17; Num. 33:52; Deut. 7:5; Deut. 12:3; Deut. 16:21; 2 Kgs.18:3, 4.

Q. 98. But may not images be tolerated in the churches, as books to the laity?

No: for we must not pretend to be wiser than God, who will have His people taught, not by dumb images,[a] but by the lively preaching of His word.[b]

[a] Jer. 10:8; Hab. 2:18, 19. [b] Rom. 10:14, 15, 17; 2 Pet. 1:19; 2 Tim. 3:16, 17.

Q. 99. What is required in the third commandment?

That we, not only by cursing[a] or perjury,[b] but also by rash swearing,[c] must not profane or abuse the name of God; nor by silence or connivance be partakers of these horrible sins in others;[d] and, briefly, that we use the holy name of God no otherwise than with fear and reverence;[e] so that He may be rightly confessed[f] and worshipped by us,[g] and be glorified in all our words and works.[h]

[a] Lev. 24:11–16. [b] Lev. 19:12. [c] Matt. 5:37; Jas. 5:12. [d] Lev. 5:1; Prov. 29:24. [e] Jer. 4:2; Isa. 45:23. [f] Rom. 10:9, 10; Matt. 10:32. [g] Ps. 50:15; 1 Tim. 2:8. [h] Rom. 2:24; 1 Tim. 6:1; Col. 3:16, 17.

Q. 100. Is then the profaning of God's name, by swearing and cursing, so heinous a sin, that His wrath is kindled against those who seek not, as much as in them lies, to hinder and forbid the same?

Yes truly:[a] for no sin is greater, or more provoking to God, than the profaning of His name. Wherefore He even commanded it to be punished with death.[b]

[a] Prov. 29:24; Lev. 5:1. [b] Lev. 24:15, 16.

Q. 101. May we then swear religiously by the name of God?

Yes: either when the magistrates demand it of the subjects; or when necessity requires us thereby to confirm a fidelity and truth to the glory of God, and the safety of our neighbor: for such an oath is founded on God's word,[a] and therefore was justly used by the saints, both in the Old and New Testament.[b]

[a] Deut. 6:13; Deut. 10:20; Isa. 48:1; Heb. 6:16. [b] Gen. 21:24; Gen. 31:53, 54; Jos. 9:15, 19; 1 Sam. 24:22; 2 Sam. 3:35; 1 Kgs. 1:28–30; Rom. 1:9; 2 Cor. 1:23.

Q. 102. May we swear by saints or any other creatures?

No; for a lawful oath is calling upon God, as the only one who knows the heart, that He will bear witness to the truth, and punish me if I swear falsely;[a] which honor is due to no creature.[b]

[a] 2 Cor. 1:23; Rom. 9:1. [b] Matt. 5:34–36; Jas. 5:12.

Q. 103. What does God require in the fourth commandment?

First, that the ministry of the gospel and the schools be maintained;[a] and that I, especially on the sabbath, that is, on the day of rest, diligently frequent the church of God,[b] to hear his word,[c] to use the sacraments,[d] publicly to call upon the Lord,[e] and contribute to the relief of the poor.[f] Secondly, that all the days of my life I cease from my evil works, and yield myself to the Lord, to work by his Holy Spirit in me: and thus begin in this life the eternal sabbath.[g]

[a] Tit. 1:5; 2 Tim. 3:14, 15; 1 Tim. 5:17; 1 Cor. 9:11, 13, 14; 2 Tim. 2:2. [b] Ps. 40:10, 11; Ps. 68:27; Acts 2:42, 46. [c] 1 Tim. 4:13, 19; 1 Cor. 14:29, 31. [d] 1 Cor. 11:33. [e] 1 Tim. 2:1–3, 8–11; 1 Cor. 14:16. [f] 1 Cor. 16:2. [g] Isa. 66:23.

Q. 104. What does God require in the fifth commandment?

That I show all honor, love, and fidelity to my father and mother, and all in authority over me, and submit myself to their good instruction and correction, with due obedience;[a] and also patiently bear with their weaknesses and infirmities,[b] since it pleases God to govern us by their hand.[c]

[a] Eph. 5:22; Eph. 6:1–5; Col. 3:18, 20–24; Prov. 1:8; Prov. 4:1; Prov. 15:20; Prov. 20:20; Exod. 21:17; Rom. 13:1–7. [b] Prov. 23:22; Gen. 9:24, 25; 1 Pet. 2:18. [c] Eph. 6:4, 9; Col. 3:19–21; Rom. 13:2, 3; Matt. 22:21.

Q. 105. What does God require in the sixth commandment?

That neither in thoughts, nor words, nor gestures, much less in deeds, I dishonor, hate, wound, or kill my neighbor, by myself or by another:[a] but that I lay aside all desire of revenge:[b] also, that I hurt not myself, nor willfully expose myself to any danger.[c] Wherefore also, to prevent murder, the magistrate is armed with the sword.[d]

[a] Matt. 5:21, 22; Matt. 26:52; Gen. 9:6. [b] Eph. 4:26; Rom. 12:19; Matt. 5:25; Matt. 18:35. [c] Rom. 13:14; Col. 2:23; Matt. 4:7. [d] Gen. 9:6; Exod. 21:14; Matt. 26:52; Rom. 13:4.

Q. 106. But this commandment speaks only of murder?

In forbidding murder, God teaches us, that He abhors the causes thereof, such as envy,[a] hatred,[b] anger,[c] and desire of revenge; and that He accounts all these as murder.[d]

[a] Prov. 14:30; Rom. 1:29. [b] 1 John 2:9, 11. [c] Jas. 1:20; Gal. 5:19, 21. [d] 1 John 3:15.

Q. 107. But is it enough that we do not kill any man in the manner mentioned above?

No: for when God forbids envy, hatred, and anger, He commands us to love our neighbor as ourselves;[a] to show patience, peace, meekness, mercy, and all kindness towards him,[b] and prevent his hurt as much as in us lies;[c] and that we do good, even to our enemies.[d]

[a] Matt. 7:12; Matt. 22:39; Rom. 12:10. [b] Eph. 4:2; Gal. 6:1, 2; Matt. 5:5, 7, 9; Rom. 12:18; Luke 6:36; 1 Pet. 3:8; Col. 3:12; Rom. 12:10, 15. [c] Exod. 23:5. [d] Matt. 5:44, 45; Rom. 12:20, 21.

Q. 108. What does the seventh commandment teach us?

That all unchastity is accursed of God:[a] and that therefore we must with all our hearts detest the same,[b] and live chastely and modestly,[c] whether in holy wedlock or in single life.[d]

[a] Lev. 18:27, 28. [b] Jude 1:23. [c] 1 Thess. 4:3–5. [d] Heb. 13:4; 1 Cor. 7:7–9, 27.

Q. 109. Does God in this commandment only forbid adultery and such like gross sins?

Since both our body and soul are temples of the Holy Ghost, He commands us to preserve them pure and holy: therefore, He forbids all unchaste actions, gestures, words,[a] thoughts, desires,[b] and whatever can entice men thereto.[c]

[a] Eph. 5:3, 4; 1 Cor. 6:18–20. [b] Matt. 5:27, 28. [c] Eph. 5:18; 1 Cor. 15:33.

Q. 110. What does God forbid in the eighth commandment?

God forbids not only those thefts,[a] and robberies,[b] which are punishable by the magistrate; but He comprehends under the name of theft all wicked tricks and devices, whereby we design to appropriate to ourselves the goods which belong to our neighbor:[c] whether it be by force, or under the appearance of right, as by unjust weights, ells,[2] measures, fraudulent merchandise,[d] false coins, usury,[e] or by any other way forbidden by God; as also all covetousness,[f] all abuse and waste of his gifts.[g]

[a] 1 Cor. 6:10. [b] 1 Cor. 5:10; Isa. 33:1. [c] Luke 3:14; 1 Thess. 4:6. [d] Prov. 11:1; Prov. 16:11; Ezek. 45:9–12; Deut. 25:13–16. [e] Ps. 15:5; Luke 6:35. [f] 1 Cor. 6:10. [g] Prov. 23:20, 21; Prov. 21:20.

[2] A former unit of measure of approximately 45 inches that was used mainly for textile.

Q. 111. But what does God require in this commandment?

That I promote the advantage of my neighbour in every instance I can or may; and deal with him as I desire to be dealt with by others:[a] further also that I faithfully labor, so that I may be able to relieve the needy.[b]

[a] Matt. 7:12. [b] Eph. 4:28.

Q. 112. What is required in the ninth commandment?

That I bear false witness against no man,[a] nor falsify any man's words;[b] that I be no backbiter, nor slanderer;[c] that I do not judge, nor join in condemning any man rashly, or unheard;[d] but that I avoid all sorts of lies and deceit, as the proper works of the devil,[e] unless I would bring down upon me the heavy wrath of God;[f] likewise, that in judgment and all other dealings I love the truth, speak it uprightly and confess it;[g] also that I defend and promote, as much as I am able, the horror and good character of my neighbor.[h]

[a] Prov. 19:5, 9; Prov. 21:28. [b] Ps. 15:3; Ps. 50:19, 20. [c] Rom. 1:29, 30. [d] Matt. 7:1, 2; Luke 6:37. [e] John 8:44. [f] Prov. 12:22; Prov. 13:5. [g] 1 Cor. 13:6; Eph. 4:25. [h] 1 Pet. 4:8.

Q. 113. What does the tenth commandment require of us?

That even the smallest inclination or thought, contrary to any of God's commandments, never rise in our hearts; but that at all times we hate all sin with our whole heart and delight in all righteousness.[a]

[a] Rom. 7:7.

Q. 114. But can those who are converted to God perfectly keep these commandments?

No: but even the holiest men, while in this life, have only a small beginning of this obedience;[a] yet so, that with a sincere resolution they begin to live, not only according to some, but all the commandments of God.[b]

[a] 1 John 1:8–10; Rom. 7:14, 15; Eccl. 7:20; 1 Cor. 13:9. [b] Rom. 7:22; Ps. 1:2; Jas. 2:10.

Q. 115. Why will God then have the Ten Commandments so strictly preached, since no man in this life can keep them?

First, that all our lifetime we may learn more and more to know[a] our sinful nature, and thus become the more earnest in seeking the remission of sin, and righteousness in Christ;[b] likewise, that we constantly endeavor and pray to God for the grace of the Holy Spirit, that we may become more and more conformable to the image of God, till we arrive at the perfection proposed to us, in a life to come.[c]

[a] Rom. 3:20; 1 John 1:9; Ps. 32:5. [b] Matt. 5:6; Rom. 7:24, 25. [c] 1 Cor. 9:24; Philip. 3:11–14.

Of Prayer

Q. 116. Why is prayer necessary for Christians?

Because it is the chief part of thankfulness which God requires of us:[a] and also, because God will give His grace and Holy Spirit to those only, who with sincere desires, continually ask them of Him and are thankful for them.[b]

[a] Ps. 50:14, 15. [b] Matt. 7:7, 8; Luke 11:9, 10, 13; 1 Thess. 5:17.

Q. 117. What are the requisites of that prayer, which is acceptable to God, and which He will hear?

First, that we from the heart pray[a] to the one true God only, who has manifested Himself in His word,[b] for all things, He has commanded us to ask of Him;[c] secondly, that we rightly and thoroughly know our need and misery,[d] that so we may deeply humble ourselves in the presence of His divine majesty;[e] thirdly, that we be fully persuaded that He, notwithstanding that we are unworthy of it, will, for the sake of Christ our Lord, certainly hear our prayer,[f] as He has promised us in His word.[g]

[a] John 4:24; Ps. 145:18. [b] Rev. 19:10; John 4:22–24. [c] Rom. 8:26; 1 John 5:14; Jas. 1:5. [d] 2 Chron. 20:12. [e] Ps. 2:11; Ps. 34:19; Isa. 66:2. [f] Rom. 10:14; Jas. 1:6. [g] John 14:13, 14; John 16:23; Dan. 9:17, 18. [h] Matt. 7:8; Ps. 27:8.

Q. 118. What has God commanded us to ask of Him?

All things necessary for soul and body,[a] which Christ our Lord has comprised in that prayer taught us by Himself.

[a] Jas. 1:17; Matt. 6:33.

Q. 119. What is the Lord's Prayer?[a]

Our Father, who art in heaven, hallowed be Thy name. Thy kingdom come. Thy will be done on earth, as it is in heaven. Give us this day our daily bread. And forgive us our debts, as we forgive our debtors. And lead us not into temptation, but deliver us from evil. For Thine is the kingdom, and the power, and the glory, for ever. Amen.

[a] Matt. 6:9–13; Luke 11:2–4.

Q. 120. Why has Christ commanded us to address God thus: "Our Father"?

That immediately, in the very beginning of our prayer, He might excite in us a childlike reverence for and confidence in God, which are the foundation of our prayer: namely, that God is become our Father in Christ and will much less deny us what we ask of Him in true faith, than our parents will refuse us earthly things.[a]

[a] Matt. 7:9–11; Luke 11:11–13.

Q. 121. Why is it here added, "Who art in heaven"?

Lest we should form any earthly conceptions of God's heavenly majesty,[a] and that we may expect from His almighty power all things necessary for soul and body.[b]

[a] Jer. 23:23, 24; Acts 17:24, 25, 27. [b] Rom. 10:12.

Q. 122. Which is the first petition?

"Hallowed be Thy name"; that is, grant us, first, rightly to know Thee,[a] and to sanctify, glorify, and praise Thee,[b] in all thy works, in which Thy power, wisdom, goodness, justice, mercy and truth are clearly displayed; and further also, that we may so order and direct our whole lives, our thoughts, words and actions, that Thy name may never be blasphemed, but rather honored and praised on our account.[c]

[a] John 17:3; Jer. 9:24; Jer. 31:33, 34; Matt. 16:17; Jas. 1:5; Ps. 119:105. [b] Ps. 119:137; Luke 1:46, 47, 68, 69; Rom. 11:33–36. [c] Ps. 71:8; Ps.115:1.

Q. 123. Which is the second petition?

"Thy kingdom come"; that is, rule us so by Thy word and Spirit, that we may submit ourselves more and more to Thee;[a] preserve and increase Thy church;[b] destroy the works of the devil, and all violence which would exalt itself against Thee; and also all wicked counsels devised against Thy holy word;[c] till the full perfection of Thy kingdom take place,[d] wherein Thou shalt be all in all.[e]

[a] Matt. 6:33; Ps. 119:5; Ps. 143:10. [b] Ps. 51:18; Ps. 122:6–9. [c] 1 John 3:8; Rom. 16:20. [d] Rev. 22:17, 20; Rom. 8:22, 23. [e] 1 Cor. 15:28.

Q. 124. Which is the third petition?

"Thy will be done on earth, as it is in heaven"; that is, grant that we and all men may renounce our own will,[a] and without murmuring obey Thy will, which is only good;[b] that every one may attend to and perform the duties of his station and calling,[c] as willingly and faithfully as the angels do in heaven.[d]

[a] Matt. 16:24; Tit. 2:11, 12. [b] Luke 22:42; Eph. 5:10; Rom. 12:2. [c] 1 Cor. 7:24. [d] Ps. 103:20, 21.

Q. 125. Which is the fourth petition?

"Give us this day our daily bread"; that is, be pleased to provide us with all things necessary for the body,[a] that we may thereby acknowledge Thee to be the only fountain of all good,[b] and that neither our care nor industry, nor even Thy gifts, can profit us without Thy blessing;[c] and therefore that we may withdraw our trust from all creatures, and place it alone in Thee.[d]

[a] Ps. 104:27, 28; Ps. 145:15, 16; Matt. 6:25, 26. [b] Jas. 1:17; Acts 14:17; Acts 17:27, 28. [c] 1 Cor. 15:58; Deut. 8:3; Ps. 37:3–5, 16; Ps. 127:1, 2. [d] Ps. 55:23; Ps. 62:11; Ps. 146:3; Jer. 17:5, 7.

Q. 126. Which is the fifth petition?

"And forgive us our debts as we forgive our debtors"; that is, be pleased for the sake of Christ's blood, not to impute to us poor sinners, our transgressions, nor that depravity, which always cleaves to us;[a] even as we feel this evidence of Thy grace in us, that it is our firm resolution from the heart to forgive our neighbor.[b]

[a] Ps. 51:1–7; Ps. 143:2; 1 John 2:1, 2; Rom. 8:1. [b] Matt. 6:14, 15.

Q. 127. Which is the sixth petition?

"And lead us not into temptation, but deliver us from evil"; that is, since we are so weak in ourselves, that we cannot stand a moment;[a] and besides this, since our mortal enemies, the devil,[b] the world,[c] and our own flesh,[d] cease not to assault us, do Thou therefore preserve and strengthen us by the power of Thy Holy Spirit, that we may not be overcome in this spiritual warfare,[e] but constantly and strenuously may resist our foes, till at last we obtain a complete victory.[f]

[a] John 15:5; Ps. 103:14. [b] 1 Pet. 5:8; Eph. 6:12. [c] John 15:19. [d] Rom. 7:23; Gal. 5:17. [e] Matt. 26:41; Mark 13:33. [f] 1 Thess. 3:13; 1 Thess. 5:23.

Q. 128. How do you close this prayer?

"For Thine is the kingdom, and the power, and the glory, forever"; that is, all these we ask of Thee, because Thou, being our King and almighty, art willing and able to give us all good;[a] and all this we pray for, that thereby not we, but Thy holy name, may be glorified for ever.[b]

[a] Rom. 10:11, 12; 2 Pet. 2:9. [b] John 14:13; Jer. 33:8, 9; Ps. 115:1.

Q. 129. What is the meaning of the word "Amen"?

"Amen" means: So shall it truly and certainly be: for my prayer is more assuredly heard of God, than I feel in my heart that I desire these things of Him.[a]

[a] 2 Cor. 1:20; 2 Tim. 2:13.

An Introduction to the Canons of Dort

The Canons of Dort

The Canons of Dort are confined to five points or "Heads of Doctrine" and exhibit what is technically called the Calvinistic system—first positively, then negatively, in the rejection of the Arminian errors.[1] Each Head of Doctrine (subdivided into Articles) is subscribed by the Dutch and foreign delegates.

First Head of Doctrine

Of Divine Predestination.—Since all men sinned in Adam and lie under the curse [according to the Augustinian system held by all the Reformers], God would have done no injustice if he had left them to their merited punishment; but in his infinite mercy he provided a salvation through the gospel of Christ, that those who believe in him may not perish, but have eternal life. That some receive the gift of faith from God and others not, proceeds from God's eternal decree of election and reprobation.

[1] The term "*rejectio errorum,*" instead of the condemnation and anathemas of the Greek and Roman Churches in dealing with heresies, indicates that Protestant orthodoxy is more liberal and charitable than the Catholic.

Election is the unchangeable purpose of God whereby, before the foundation of the world, he has, out of mere grace, according to the sovereign good pleasure of his own will, chosen from the whole human race, which has fallen through their own fault from their primitive state of rectitude into sin and destruction, a certain number of persons to redemption in Christ, whom he from eternity appointed the Mediator and Head of the elect, and the foundation of salvation. These elect, though neither better nor more deserving than others, God has decreed to give to Christ to be saved by him, and bestow upon them true faith, conversion, justification and sanctification, perseverance to the end, and final glory (Eph. 1:4–6; Rom. 8:30).

Election is absolute and unconditional. It is not founded upon foreseen faith and holiness, as the prerequisite condition on which it depended; on the contrary, it is the fountain of faith, holiness, and eternal life itself. God has chosen us, not *because* we are holy, but to the *end* that we should be holy (Eph. 1:4; Rom. 9:11–13; Acts 13:38). As God is unchangeable, so his election is unchangeable, and the elect can neither be cast away nor their number be diminished. The sense and certainty of election is a constant stimulus to humility and gratitude.

The non-elect are simply left to the just condemnation of their own sins. This is the decree of reprobation, which by no means makes God the author of sin (the very thought of which is blasphemy), but declares him to be an awful, irreprehensible, and righteous judge and avenger (*Cat.* Ch. I. Art. 15).

Second Head of Doctrine

Of the Death of Christ. [Limited Atonement.]—According to the sovereign counsel of God, the saving efficacy of the atoning death of Christ extends to all the elect [and to them only], so as to bring them infallibly to salvation. But, intrinsically, the sacrifice and satisfaction of Christ is of infinite worth and value, abundantly sufficient to expiate the sins of the whole world. This death derives its infinite value and dignity from these considerations; because the person who submitted to it was not only really man and perfectly holy, but also the only-begotten Son of God, of the same eternal and infinite essence with the Father and Holy Spirit, which qualifications were necessary to constitute him a Saviour for us; and because it was attended with a sense of the wrath and curse of God due to us for sin.

Moreover, the promise of the gospel is, that whosoever believeth in Christ crucified shall not perish, but have everlasting life. This promise, together with the command to repent and believe, ought to be declared and published to all nations, and to all persons promiscuously and without distinction, to whom God out of his good pleasure sends the gospel.

And, whereas many who are called by the gospel do not repent nor believe in Christ, but perish in unbelief; this is not owing to any defect or insufficiency in the sacrifice offered by Christ upon the cross, but is wholly to be imputed to themselves.[2]

[2] The advocates of a limited atonement reason from the effect to the cause, and make the divine intention co-extensive with the actual application; but they can give no satisfactory explanation of such passages as John 3:16 ("God so loved the *world,*" which never means the elect only, but all mankind); 1 John 2:2 ("Christ is the propitiation for our sins, and *not for ours only, but also* for the sins of the *whole world*"); 1 Tim. 2:4; 2 Pet. 3:9. All admit, however, with the Articles of Dort, that the intrinsic value of the atonement, being the act of the God-man, is infinite and sufficient to cover the sins of all men. Dr. W. Cunningham says: "The value or worth of Christ's sacrifice of himself depends upon, and is measured by, the dignity of his person, and is therefore

Third and Fourth Heads of Doctrine

Of the Corruption of Man, his Conversion to God, and the Manner thereof.—Man was originally formed after the image of God. His understanding was adorned with a true and saving knowledge of his Creator, and of spiritual things; his heart and will were upright, all his affections pure, and the whole Man was holy; but revolting from God by the instigation of the devil, and abusing the freedom of his own will, he forfeited these excellent gifts, and on the contrary entailed on himself blindness of mind, horrible darkness, vanity, and perverseness of judgment; became wicked, rebellious, and obdurate in heart and will, and impure in [all] his affections.

Man after the fall begat children in his own likeness. A corrupt stock produced a corrupt offspring. Hence, all the posterity of Adam—Christ the single exception—have derived corruption from their original parent, not by imitation, as the Pelagians of old asserted, but by the propagation of a vicious nature in consequence of a just judgment of God.

Therefore, all men are conceived in sin, and are by nature children of wrath, incapable of any saving good, prone to evil, dead in sin, and in bondage thereto; and, without the regenerating

infinite. Though many fewer of the human race had been to be pardoned and saved, an atonement of infinite value would have been necessary, in order to procure for them these blessings; and though many more, yea, all men, had been to be pardoned and saved, the death of Christ, being an atonement of infinite value, would have been amply sufficient, as the ground or basis of their forgiveness or salvation" (*Historical Theol.* Vol. II. p. 331). Similarly, Dr. Hodge, Vol. II. pp. 544 sqq. After such admissions the difference of the two theories is of little practical account. Full logical consistency would require us to measure the value of Christ's atonement by the extent of its actual benefit or availability, and either to expand or to contract it according to the number of the elect; but such an opinion is derogatory to the dignity of Christ, and is held by very few extreme Calvinists of little or no influence. Cunningham says (p. 331): "There is no doubt that all the most eminent Calvinistic divines hold the infinite worth or value of Christ's atonement—its full sufficiency for expiating all the sins of all men."

grace of the Holy Spirit, they are neither able nor willing to return to God, to reform the depravity of their nature, nor to dispose themselves to reformation.

What, therefore, neither the light of nature nor the law could do, that God performs by the operation of his Holy Spirit through the word or ministry of reconciliation: which is the glad tidings concerning the Messiah, by means whereof it hath pleased God to save such as believe, as well under the Old as under the New Testament.

As many as are called by the gospel are unfeignedly called; for God hath most earnestly and truly declared in his Word what will be acceptable to him, namely, that all who are called should comply with the invitation. He, moreover, seriously promises eternal life and rest to as many as shall come to him, and believe on him.

It is not the fault of the gospel, nor of Christ offered therein, nor of God, who calls men by the gospel, and confers upon them various gifts, that those who are called by the ministry of the Word refuse to come and be converted. The fault lies in themselves.

But that others who are called by the gospel obey the call must be wholly ascribed to God, who, as he hath chosen his own from eternity in Christ, so he calls them effectually in time, confers upon them faith and repentance, rescues them from the power of darkness, and translates them into the kingdom of his own Son, that they may show forth the praises of him who hath called them out of darkness into his marvelous light; and may glory not in themselves but in the Lord, according to the testimony of the Apostles in various places.

Faith is therefore the gift of God, not on account of its being offered by God to man, to be accepted or rejected at his pleasure, but because it is in reality conferred, breathed, and infused into him; nor even because God bestows the power or ability to believe, and then expects that man should, by the exercise of his own free will, consent to the terms of salvation, and actually believe in Christ; but because he who works in man both to will and to do, and indeed all things in all, produces both the will to believe and the act of believing also.

Fifth Head of Doctrine

Of the Perseverance of the Saints.—Whom God calls, according to his purpose, to the communion of his Son our Lord Jesus Christ, and regenerates by the Holy Spirit, he delivers also from the dominion and slavery of sin in this life; though not altogether from the body of sin and from the infirmities of the flesh, so long as they continue in this world.

By reason of these remains of indwelling sin, and the temptations of sin and of the world, those who are converted could not persevere in a state of grace if left to their own strength. But God is faithful, who having conferred grace, mercifully confirms and powerfully preserves them therein, even to the end.

Of this preservation of the elect to salvation, and of their perseverance in the faith, true believers for themselves may and do obtain assurance according to the measure of their faith, whereby they arrive at the certain persuasion that they ever will continue true and living members of the Church; and that they experience forgiveness of sins, and will at last inherit eternal life.

This certainty of perseverance, however, is so far from exciting in believers a spirit of pride, or of rendering them carnally secure, that, on the contrary, it is the real source of humility, filial reverence, true piety, patience in every tribulation, fervent prayers, constancy in suffering and in confessing the truth, and of solid rejoicing in God; so that the consideration of this benefit should serve as an incentive to the serious and constant practice of gratitude and good works, as appears from the testimonies of Scripture and the examples of the saints.

* * *

In opposition to the Canons of Dort, Episcopius prepared a lengthy defense of the Arminian Articles and a confession of faith in Dutch, 1621, and in Latin, 1622. It claims no binding symbolical authority and advocates liberty and toleration.[3]

[3] A German translation in Böckel's *Bekenntniss-Schriften*, pp. 545–640.

The Canons of Dort
(1618–1619)

First Head of Doctrine

Of Divine Predestination

Article 1. As all men have sinned in Adam, lie under the curse, and are deserving of eternal death, God would have done no injustice by leaving them all to perish, and delivering them over to condemnation on account of sin, according to the words of the apostle, Romans 3:19, "that every mouth may be stopped, and all the world may become guilty before God." And verse 23: "for all have sinned, and come short of the glory of God." And Romans 6:23: "for the wages of sin is death."

Article 2. But in this the love of God was manifested, that he sent his only begotten Son into the world, that whosoever believeth on him should not perish, but have everlasting life (1 John 4:9; John 3:16).

Article 3. And that men may be brought to believe, God mercifully sends the messengers of these most joyful tidings, to whom he will and at what time he pleaseth; by whose ministry men are called to repentance and faith in Christ crucified. Romans 10:14, 15: "How then shall they call on him in whom they have not believed? and how shall they believe in him of whom they have not heard? And how shall they hear without a preacher? And how shall they preach except they be sent?"

Article 4. The wrath of God abideth upon those who believe not this gospel. But such as receive it, and embrace Jesus the Savior by a true and living faith, are by him delivered from the wrath of God, and from destruction, and have the gift of eternal life conferred upon them.

Article 5. The cause or guilt of this unbelief, as well as of all other sins, is no wise in God, but in man himself; whereas faith in Jesus Christ, and salvation through him is the free gift of God, as it is written: "By grace ye are saved through faith, and that not of yourselves, it is the gift of God," Ephesians 2:8. "And unto you it is given in the behalf of Christ, not only to believe on him," etc. Philippians 1:29.

Article 6. That some receive the gift of faith from God, and others do not receive it proceeds from God's eternal decree, "For known unto God are all his works from the beginning of the world," Acts 15:18. "Who worketh all things after the counsel of his will," Ephesians 1:11. According to which decree, he graciously softens the hearts of the elect, however obstinate, and inclines them to believe, while he leaves the non-elect in his just judgment to their own wickedness and obduracy. And herein is especially displayed the profound and merciful and, at the same time, the righteous discrimination between men, equally involved in ruin; or that decree of election and reprobation, revealed in the Word of God, which though men of perverse, impure and unstable minds wrest to their own destruction, yet to holy and pious souls affords unspeakable consolation.

Article 7. Election is the unchangeable purpose of God, whereby, before the foundation of the world, he hath out of mere grace, according to the sovereign good pleasure of his own will, chosen, from the whole human race, which had fallen through their own fault, from their primitive state of rectitude, into sin and destruction, a certain number of persons to redemption in Christ, whom he from eternity appointed the Mediator and Head of the elect, and the foundation of Salvation.

This elect number, though by nature neither better nor more deserving than the others, but with them involved in one common misery, God hath decreed to give to Christ, to be saved by him, and effectually to call and draw them to his communion by his Word and Spirit, to bestow upon them true faith, justification, and sanctification; and having powerfully preserved them in the fellowship of his Son, finally, to glorify them for the demonstration of his mercy, and for the praise of his glorious grace; as it is written: "According as he hath chosen us in him, before the foundation of the world, that we should be holy, and without blame before him in love; having predestinated us unto the adoption of children by Jesus Christ to himself, according to the good pleasure of his will, to the praise of the glory of his grace, wherein he hath made us accepted in the beloved," Ephesians 1:4–6. And elsewhere: "Whom he did predestinate, them he also called; and whom he called, them he also justified; and whom he justified, them he also glorified," Romans 8:30.

Article 8. There are not various decrees of election, but one and the same decree respecting all those, who shall be saved, both under the Old and New Testament: since the Scripture declares the good pleasure, purpose, and counsel of the divine will to be one, according to which he hath chosen us from eternity, both to grace and glory, to salvation, and the way of salvation, which he hath ordained that we should walk therein.

Article 9. This election was not founded upon foreseen faith, and the obedience of faith, holiness, or any other good quality of disposition in man, as the pre-requisite, cause or condition on which it depended; but men are chosen to faith and to the obedience of faith, holiness, etc. Therefore, election is the fountain of every saving good; from which proceed faith, holiness, and the other gifts of salvation, and finally eternal life itself, as its fruits and effects, according to that of the apostle: "He hath chosen us (not because we were) but that we should be holy, and without blame, before him in love," Ephesians 1:4.

Article 10. The good pleasure of God is the sole cause of this gracious election; which doth not consist herein, that out of all possible qualities and actions of men God has chosen some as a condition of salvation; but that he was pleased out of the common mass of sinners to adopt some certain persons as a peculiar people to himself, as it is written, "For the children being not yet born neither having done any good or evil," etc., it was said (namely to Rebecca): "the elder shall serve the younger; as it is written, Jacob have I loved, but Esau have I hated," Romans 9:11–13. "And as many as were ordained to eternal life believed," Acts 13:48.

Article 11. And as God himself is most wise, unchangeable, omniscient and omnipotent, so the election made by him can neither be interrupted nor changed, recalled or annulled; neither can the elect be cast away, nor their number diminished.

Article 12. The elect in due time, though in various degrees and in different measures, attain the assurance of this their eternal and unchangeable election, not by inquisitively prying into the secret and deep things of God, but by observing in themselves with a spiritual joy and holy pleasure, the infallible fruits of election pointed out in the Word of God—such as a true faith in Christ, filial fear, a godly sorrow for sin, a hungering and thirsting after righteousness, etc.

Article 13. The sense and certainty of this election afford to the children of God additional matter for daily humiliation before him, for adoring the depth of his mercies, for cleansing themselves, and rendering grateful returns of ardent love to him, who first manifested so great love towards them. The consideration of this doctrine of election is so far from encouraging remissness in the observance of the divine commands, or from sinking men in carnal security, that these, in the just judgment of God, are the usual effects of rash presumption, or of idle and wanton trifling with the grace of election, in those who refuse to walk in the ways of the elect.

Article 14. As the doctrine of divine election by the most wise counsel of God, was declared by the prophets, by Christ himself, and by the apostles, and is clearly revealed in the Scriptures, both of the Old and New Testament, so it is still to be published in due time and place in the Church of God, for which it was peculiarly designed, provided it be done with reverence, in the spirit of discretion and piety, for the glory of God's most holy name, and for enlivening and comforting his people, without vainly attempting to investigate the secret ways of the Most High, Acts 20:27;Romans 11:33, 34;12:3; Hebrews 6:17, 18.

Article 15. What peculiarly tends to illustrate and recommend to us the eternal and unmerited grace of election is the express testimony of sacred Scripture, that not all, but some only are elected, while others are passed by in the eternal election of God; whom God, out of his sovereign, most just, irreprehensible, and unchangeable good pleasure, hath decreed to leave in the common misery into which they have willfully plunged themselves, and not to bestow upon them saving faith and the grace of conversion; but leaving them in his just judgment to follow their own ways, at last for the declaration of his justice, to condemn and punish them forever, not only on account of their unbelief, but also for all their other sins. And this is the decree of reprobation which by no means makes God the author of sin (the very thought of which is blasphemy), but declares him to be an awful, irreprehensible, and righteous judge and avenger thereof.

Article 16. Those who do not yet experience a lively faith in Christ, an assured confidence of soul, peace of conscience, an earnest endeavor after filial obedience, and glorying in God through Christ, efficaciously wrought in them, and do nevertheless persist in the use of the means which God hath appointed for working these graces in us, ought not to be alarmed at the mention of reprobation, nor to rank themselves among the reprobate, but diligently to persevere in the use of means, and with ardent desires, devoutly and humbly to wait for a season of richer grace. Much less cause have they to be terrified by the doctrine of reprobation, who, though they seriously desire to be turned to God, to please him only, and to be delivered from the body of death, cannot yet reach that measure of holiness and faith to which they aspire; since a merciful God has promised that he will not quench the smoking flax, nor break the bruised reed. But this doctrine is justly terrible to those, who, regardless of God and of the Savior Jesus Christ, have wholly given themselves up to the cares of the world, and the pleasures of the flesh, so long as they are not seriously converted to God.

Article 17. Since we are to judge of the will of God from his Word, which testifies that the children of believers are holy, not by nature, but in virtue of the covenant of grace, in which they, together with the parents, are comprehended, godly parents have no reason to doubt of the election and salvation of their children, whom it pleaseth God to call out of this life in their infancy.

Article 18. To those who murmur at the free grace of election, and just severity of reprobation, we answer with the apostle: "Nay, but, O man, who art thou that repliest against God?" Romans 9:20 and quote the language of our Savior: "Is it not lawful for me to do what I will with my own?" Matthew 20:15. And therefore with holy adoration of these mysteries, we exclaim in the words of the apostle: "O the depths of the riches both of the wisdom and knowledge of God! how unsearchable are his judgments, and his ways past finding out! For who hath known the mind of the Lord, or who hath been his counselor? or who hath first given to him, and it shall be recompensed unto him again? For of him, and through him, and to him are all things: to whom be glory for ever. Amen."

* * *

Rejection of Errors

The true doctrine concerning Election and Reprobation having been explained, the Synod rejects the errors of those:

I. Who teach: That the will of God to save those who would believe and would persevere in faith and in the obedience of faith, is the whole and entire decree of election unto salvation, and that nothing else concerning this decree has been revealed in God's Word.

For these deceive the simple and plainly contradict the Scriptures, which declare that God will not only save those who will believe, but that he has also from eternity chosen certain particular persons to whom above others he in time will grant both faith in Christ and perseverance; as it written: "I manifested thy name unto the men whom thou gavest me out of the world," John 17:6. "And as many as were ordained to eternal life believed," Acts 13:48. And: "Even as he chose us in him before the foundation of the world, that we should be holy and without blemish before him in love," Ephesians 1:4.

II. Who teach: That there are various kinds of election of God unto eternal life: the one general and indefinite, the other particular and definite; and that the latter in turn is either incomplete, revocable, non-decisive and conditional, or complete, irrevocable, decisive and absolute. Likewise: that there is one election unto faith, and another unto salvation, so that election can be unto justifying faith, without being a decisive election unto salvation. For this is a fancy of men's minds, invented regardless of the Scriptures, whereby the doctrine of election is corrupted, and this golden chain of our salvation is broken: "And whom he foreordained, them he also called; and whom he called, them he also justified; and whom he justified, them he also glorified," Romans 8:30.

III. Who teach: That the good pleasure and purpose of God, of which Scripture makes mention in the doctrine of election, does not consist in this, that God chose certain persons rather than others, but in this that he chose out of all possible conditions (among which are also the works of the law), or out of the whole order of things, the act of faith which from its very nature is undeserving, as well as its incomplete obedience, as a condition of salvation, and that he would graciously consider this in itself as a complete obedience and count it worthy of the reward of eternal life. For by this injurious error the pleasure of God and the merits of Christ are made of none effect, and men are drawn away by useless questions from the truth of gracious justification and from the simplicity of Scripture, and this declaration of the Apostle is charged as untrue: "Who saved us, and called us with a holy calling, not according to our works, but according to his own purpose and grace, which was given us in Christ Jesus before times eternal," 2 Timothy 1:9.

IV. Who teach: That in the election unto faith this condition is beforehand demanded, namely, that man should use the light of nature aright, be pious, humble, meek, and fit for eternal life, as if on these things election were in any way dependent.

For this savors of the teaching of Pelagius, and is opposed to the doctrine of the apostle, when he writes: "Among whom we also all once lived in the lust of our flesh, doing the desires of the flesh and of the mind, and were by nature children of wrath, even as the rest; but God being rich in mercy, for his great love wherewith he loved us, even when we were dead through our trespasses, made us alive together with Christ (by grace have ye been saved), and raised us up with him, and made us to sit with him in heavenly places, in Christ Jesus, that in the ages to come he might show the exceeding riches of his grace in kindness towards us in Christ Jesus; for by grace have ye been saved through faith; and that not of yourselves, it is the gift of God; not of works, that no man should glory," Ephesians 2:3–9.

V. Who teach: That the incomplete and non-decisive election of particular persons to salvation occurred because of a foreseen faith, conversion, holiness, godliness, which either began or continued for some time; but that the complete and decisive election occurred because of foreseen perseverance unto the end in faith, conversion, holiness and godliness; and that this is the gracious and evangelical worthiness, for the sake of which he who is chosen, is more worthy than he who is not chosen; and that therefore faith, the obedience of faith, holiness, godliness and perseverance are not fruits of the unchangeable election unto glory, but are conditions, which, being required beforehand, were foreseen as being met by those who will be fully elected, and are causes without which the unchangeable election to glory does not occur.

This is repugnant to the entire Scripture, which constantly inculcates this and similar declarations: Election is not out of works, but of him that calleth, Romans 9:11. "As many as were ordained to eternal life believed," Acts 13:48. "He chose us in him before the foundation of the world, that we should be holy," Ephesians 1:4. "Ye did not choose me, but I chose you," John 15:16. "But if it be of grace, it is no more of works," Romans 11:6. "Herein is love, not that we loved God, but that he loved us, and sent his Son," 1 John 4:10.

VI. Who teach: That not every election unto salvation is unchangeable, but that some of the elect, any decree of God notwithstanding, can yet perish and do indeed perish. By which gross error they make God to be changeable, and destroy the comfort which the godly obtain out of the firmness of their election, and contradict the Holy Scripture, which teaches, that the elect can not be lead astray, Matthew 24:24; that Christ does not lose those whom the Father gave him, John 6:39; and that God hath also glorified those whom he foreordained, called and justified, Romans 8:30.

VII. Who teach: That there is in this life no fruit and no consciousness of the unchangeable election to glory, nor any certainty, except that which depends on a changeable and uncertain condition. For not only is it absurd to speak of an uncertain certainty, but also contrary to the experience of the saints, who by virtue of the consciousness of their election rejoice with the Apostle and praise this favor of God, Ephesians 1; who according to Christ's admonition rejoice with his disciples that their names are written in heaven, Luke 10:20; who also place the consciousness of their election over against the fiery darts of the devil, asking: "Who shall lay anything to the charge of God's elect?" Romans 8:33.

VIII. Who teach: That God, simply by virtue of his righteous will, did not decide either to leave anyone in the fall of Adam and in the common state of sin and condemnation, or to pass anyone by in the communication of grace which is necessary for faith and conversion. For this is firmly decreed: "He hath mercy on whom he will, and whom he will he hardeneth," Romans 9:18. And also this: "Unto you it is given to know the mysteries of the kingdom of heaven, but to them it is not given," Matthew 13:11. Likewise: "I thank thee, O Father, Lord of heaven and earth, that thou didst hide these things from the wise and understanding, and didst reveal them unto babes; yea, Father, for so it was well-pleasing in thy sight," Matthew 11:25, 26.

IX. Who teach: That the reason why God sends the gospel to one people rather than to another is not merely and solely the good pleasure of God, but rather the fact that one people is better and worthier than another to whom the gospel is not communicated. For this Moses denies, addressing the people of Israel as follows: "Behold unto Jehovah thy God belongeth heaven and the heaven of heavens, the earth, with all that is therein. Only Jehovah had a delight in thy fathers to love him, and he chose their seed after them, even you above all peoples, as at this day," Deuteronomy 10:14, 15. And Christ said: "Woe unto thee, Chorazin! woe unto thee, Bethsaida! for if the might works had been done in Tyre and

Sidon which were done in you, they would have repented long ago in sackcloth and ashes," Matthew 11:21.

Second Head of Doctrine

OF THE DEATH OF CHRIST,
AND THE REDEMPTION OF MEN THEREBY

Article 1. God is not only supremely merciful, but also supremely just. And his justice requires (as he hath revealed himself in his Word), that our sins committed against his infinite majesty should be punished, not only with temporal, but with eternal punishment, both in body and soul; which we cannot escape, unless satisfaction be made to the justice of God.

Article 2. Since therefore we are unable to make that satisfaction in our own persons, or to deliver ourselves from the wrath of God, he hath been pleased in his infinite mercy to give his only begotten Son, for our surety, who was made sin, and became a curse for us and in our stead, that he might make satisfaction to divine justice on our behalf.

Article 3. The death of the Son of God is the only and most perfect sacrifice and satisfaction for sin; and is of infinite worth and value, abundantly sufficient to expiate the sins of the whole world.

Article 4. This death derives its infinite value and dignity from these considerations, because the person who submitted to it was not only really man, and perfectly holy, but also the only begotten

Son of God, of the same eternal and infinite essence with the Father and the Holy Spirit, which qualifications were necessary to constitute him a Savior for us; and because it was attended with a sense of the wrath and curse of God due to us for sin.

Article 5. Moreover, the promise of the gospel is that whosoever believeth in Christ crucified shall not perish, but have everlasting life. This promise, together with the command to repent and believe, ought to be declared and published to all nations and to all persons promiscuously and without distinction, to whom God out of his good pleasure sends the gospel.

Article 6. And, whereas many who are called by the gospel, do not repent, nor believe in Christ, but perish in unbelief; this is not owing to any defect or insufficiency in the sacrifice offered by Christ upon the cross, but is wholly to be imputed to themselves.

Article 7. But as many as truly believe and are delivered and saved from sin and destruction through the death of Christ, are indebted for this benefit solely to the grace of God, given them in Christ from everlasting and not to any merit of their own.

Article 8. For this was the sovereign counsel and most gracious will and purpose of God the Father: that the quickening and saving efficacy of the most precious death of his Son should extend to all the elect, for bestowing upon them alone the gift of justifying faith, thereby to bring them infallibly to salvation: that is, it was the will of God that Christ, by the blood of the cross, whereby he confirmed the new covenant, should effectually redeem out of every people, tribe, nation, and language, all those, and those only, who were from eternity chosen to salvation, and given to him by the Father; that he should confer upon them faith, which together with all the other saving gifts of the Holy Spirit, he purchased for them by his death; should purge them from all sin, both original and actual, whether committed before or after believing; and having faithfully preserved them even to the end, should at last bring them free from every spot and blemish to the enjoyment of glory in his own presence forever.

Article 9. This purpose proceeding from everlasting love towards the elect, has from the beginning of the world to this day been powerfully accomplished, and will henceforward still continue to be accomplished, notwithstanding all the ineffectual opposition of the gates of hell, so that the elect in due time may be gathered together into one, and that there never may be wanting a church composed of believers, the foundation of which is laid in the blood of Christ, which may steadfastly love, and faithfully serve him as their Savior, who as a bridegroom for his bride, laid down his life for them upon the cross, and which may celebrate his praises here and through all eternity.

* * *

Rejection of Errors

The true doctrine having been explained, the Synod rejects the errors of those:

I. Who teach: That God the Father has ordained his Son to the death of the cross without a certain and definite decree to save any, so that the necessity, profitableness, and worth of what

Christ merited by his death might have existed, and might remain in all its parts complete, perfect and intact, even if the merited redemption had never in fact been applied to any person. For this doctrine tends to the despising of the wisdom of the Father and of the merits of Jesus Christ and is contrary to Scripture. For thus saith our Savior: "I lay down my life for the sheep, and I know them," John 10:15, 27. And the prophet Isaiah saith concerning the Savior: "When thou shalt make his soul an offering for sin, he shall see his seed, he shall prolong his days, and the pleasure of Jehovah shall prosper in his hand," Isaiah 53:10. Finally, this contradicts the article of faith according to which we believe the catholic Christian church.

II. Who teach: That it was not the purpose of the death of Christ that he should confirm the new covenant of grace through his blood, but only that he should acquire for the Father the mere right to establish with man such a covenant as he might please, whether of grace or of works. For this is repugnant to Scripture which teaches that Christ has become the Surety and Mediator of a better, that is, the new covenant, and that a testament is of force where death has occurred, Hebrews 7:22; 9:15, 17.

III. Who teach: That Christ by his satisfaction merited neither salvation itself for anyone, nor faith, whereby this satisfaction of Christ unto salvation is effectually appropriated; but that he merited for the Father only the authority or the perfect will to deal again with man, and to prescribe new conditions as he might desire, obedience to which, however, depended on the free will of man, so that it therefore might have come to pass that either none or all should fulfill these conditions. For these adjudge too contemptuously of the death of Christ, do in no wise acknowledge the most important fruit or benefit thereby gained, and bring again out of hell the Pelagian error.

IV. Who teach: That the new covenant of grace, which God the Father through the mediation of the death of Christ, made with man, does not herein consist that we by faith, in as much as it accepts the merits of Christ, are justified before God and saved, but in the fact that God having revoked the demand of perfect obedience of the law, regards faith itself and the obedience of faith, although imperfect, as the perfect obedience of the law, and does esteem it worthy of the reward of eternal life through grace. For these contradict the Scriptures: "Being justified freely by his grace through the redemption that is in Christ Jesus: whom God hath set forth to be a propitiation through faith in his blood," Romans 3:24, 25. And these proclaim, as did the wicked Socinus, a new and strange justification of man before God, against the consensus of the whole church.

V. Who teach: That all men have been accepted unto the state of reconciliation and unto the grace of the covenant, so that no one is worthy of condemnation on account of original sin, and that no one shall be condemned because of it, but that all are free from the guilt of original sin. For this opinion is repugnant to Scripture, which teaches that we are by nature children of wrath, Ephesians 2:3.

VI. Who use the difference between meriting and appropriating, to the end that they may instill into the minds of the imprudent and inexperienced this teaching that God, as far as he is concerned, has been minded of applying to all equally the benefits gained by the death of Christ; but that, while some obtain the pardon of sin and eternal life, and others do not, this difference depends on their own free will, which joins itself to the grace that is offered without exception, and that it is not dependent on the special gift of mercy, which powerfully works in them, that they rather than others should appropriate unto themselves this grace. For these, while they feign that they present this distinction, in a sound sense, seek to instill into the people the destructive poison of the Pelagian errors.

VII. Who teach: That Christ neither could die, needed to die, nor did die for those whom God loved in the highest degree and elected to eternal life, and did not die for these, since these do not need the death of Christ. For they contradict the Apostle, who declares: "Christ loved me, and gave himself for me," Galatians 2:20. Likewise: "Who shall lay any thing to the charge of God's elect? It is God that justifieth; who is he that condemneth? It is Christ Jesus that died," Romans 8:33, 34, namely, for them; and the Savior who says: "I lay down my life for the sheep," John 10:15. And: "This is my commandment, that ye love one another, even as I have loved you. Greater love hath no man than this, that a man lay down his life for his friends," John 15:12, 13.

Third & Fourth Heads of Doctrine

Of the Corruption of Man, His Conversion to God, and the Manner Thereof

Article 1. Man was originally formed after the image of God. His understanding was adorned with a true and saving knowledge of his Creator, and of spiritual things; his heart and will were upright; all his affections pure; and the whole man was holy; but revolting from God by the instigation of the devil, and abusing the freedom of his own will, he forfeited these excellent gifts; and on the contrary entailed on himself blindness of mind, horrible darkness, vanity and perverseness of judgment, became wicked, rebellious, and obdurate in heart and will, and impure in his affections.

Article 2. Man after the fall begat children in his own likeness. A corrupt stock produced a corrupt offspring. Hence all the posterity of Adam, Christ only excepted, have derived corruption from their original parent, not by imitation, as the Pelagians of old asserted, but by the propagation of a vicious nature.

Article 3. Therefore, all men are conceived in sin, and by nature children of wrath, incapable of saving good, prone to evil, dead in sin, and in bondage thereto, and without the regenerating grace of the Holy Spirit, they are neither able nor willing to return to God, to reform the depravity of their nature, nor to dispose themselves to reformation.

Article 4. There remain, however, in man since the fall, the glimmerings of natural light, whereby he retains some knowledge of God, of natural things, and of the differences between good and evil, and discovers some regard for virtue, good order in society, and for maintaining an orderly external deportment. But so far is this light of nature from being sufficient to bring him to a saving knowledge of God, and to true conversion, that he is incapable of using it aright even in things natural and civil. Nay further, this light, such as it is, man in various ways renders wholly polluted, and holds it in unrighteousness, by doing which he becomes inexcusable before God.

Article 5. In the same light are we to consider the law of the decalogue, delivered by God to his peculiar people the Jews, by the hands of Moses. For though it discovers the greatness of sin, and more and more convinces man thereof, yet as it neither points out a remedy, nor imparts strength to extricate him from misery, and thus being weak through the flesh, leaves the transgressor under the curse, man cannot by this law obtain saving grace.

Article 6. What therefore neither the light of nature, nor the law could do, that God performs by the operation of the Holy Spirit through the word or ministry of reconciliation: which is the glad tidings concerning the Messiah, by means whereof, it hath pleased God to save such as believe, as well under the Old, as under the New Testament.

Article 7. This mystery of his will God discovered to but a small number under the Old Testament; under the New, (the distinction between various peoples having been removed), he reveals himself to many, without any distinction of people. The cause of this dispensation is not to be ascribed to the superior worth of one nation above another, nor to their making a better use of the light of nature, but results wholly from the sovereign good pleasure and unmerited love of God. Hence, they, to whom so great and so gracious a blessing is communicated, above their desert, or rather notwithstanding their demerits, are bound to acknowledge it with humble and grateful hearts and with the apostle to adore, not curiously to pry into the severity and justice of God's judgments displayed to others, to whom this grace is not given.

Article 8. As many as are called by the gospel, are unfeignedly called. For God hath most earnestly and truly shown in his Word, what is pleasing to him, namely, that those who are called should come to him. He, moreover, seriously promises eternal life, and rest, to as many as shall come to him, and believe on him.

Article 9. It is not the fault of the gospel, nor of Christ, offered therein, nor of God, who calls men by the gospel, and confers upon them various gifts, that those who are called by the ministry of the word, refuse to come, and be converted: the fault lies in themselves; some of whom when called, regardless of their danger, reject the word of life; others, though they receive it, suffer it not to make a lasting impression on their heart; therefore, their joy, arising only from a temporary faith, soon vanishes, and they fall away; while others choke the seed of the word by perplexing cares, and the pleasures of this world, and produce no fruit. This our Savior teaches in the parable of the sower, Matthew 13.

Article 10. But that others who are called by the gospel, obey the call, and are converted, is not to be ascribed to the proper exercise of free will, whereby one distinguishes himself above others, equally furnished with grace sufficient for faith and conversions, as the proud heresy of Pelagius maintains; but it must be wholly ascribed to God, who as he has chosen his own from eternity in Christ, so he confers upon them faith and repentance, rescues them from the power of darkness, and translates them into the kingdom of his own Son, that they may show forth the praises of him, who hath called them out of darkness into his marvelous light; and may glory not in themselves, but in the Lord according to the testimony of the apostles in various places.

Article 11. But when God accomplishes his good pleasure in the elect, or works in them true conversion, he not only causes the gospel to be externally preached to them, and powerfully illumines their minds by his Holy Spirit, that they may rightly understand and discern the things of the Spirit of God; but by the efficacy of the same regenerating Spirit, pervades the inmost recesses of the man; he opens the closed, and softens the hardened heart, and circumcises that which was uncircumcised, infuses new qualities into the will, which though heretofore dead, he quickens; from being evil, disobedient and refractory, he renders it good, obedient, and pliable; actuates and strengthens it, that like a good tree, it may bring forth the fruits of good actions.

Article 12. And this is the regeneration so highly celebrated in Scripture, and denominated a new creation: a resurrection from the dead, a making alive, which God works in us without our aid. But this is in no wise effected merely by the external preaching of the gospel, by moral suasion, or such a mode of operation, that after God has performed his part, it still remains in the power of man to be regenerated or not, to be converted, or to continue unconverted; but it is evidently a supernatural work, most powerful, and at the same time most delightful, astonishing, mysterious, and ineffable; not inferior in efficacy to creation, or the resurrection from the dead, as the Scripture inspired by the author of this work declares; so that all in whose heart God works in this marvelous manner, are certainly, infallibly, and effectually regenerated, and do actually believe. Whereupon the will thus renewed, is not only actuated and influenced by God, but in consequence of this influence, becomes itself active. Wherefore also, man is himself rightly said to believe and repent, by virtue of that grace received.

Article 13. The manner of this operation cannot be fully comprehended by believers in this life. Notwithstanding which, they rest satisfied with knowing and experiencing, that by this grace of God they are enabled to believe with the heart, and love their Savior.

Article 14. Faith is therefore to be considered as the gift of God, not on account of its being offered by God to man, to be accepted or rejected at his pleasure; but because it is in reality conferred, breathed, and infused into him; or even because God bestows the power or ability to believe, and then expects that man should by the exercise of his own free will, consent to the terms of that salvation, and actually believe in Christ; but because he who works in man both to will and to do, and indeed all things in all, produces both the will to believe, and the act of believing also.

Article 15. God is under no obligation to confer this grace upon any; for how can he be indebted to man, who had no precious gifts to bestow, as a foundation for such recompense? Nay, who has nothing of his own but sin and falsehood? He therefore who becomes the subject of this grace, owes eternal gratitude to God, and gives him thanks forever. Whoever is not made partaker thereof, is either altogether regardless of these spiritual gifts, and satisfied with his own condition; or is in no apprehension of danger, and vainly boasts the possession of that which he has not. With respect to those who make an external profession of faith, and live regular lives, we are bound, after the example of the apostle, to judge and speak of them in the most favorable manner. For the secret recesses of the heart are unknown to us. And as to others, who have not yet been called, it is our duty to pray for them to God, who calls the things that are not, as if they were. But we are in no wise to conduct ourselves towards them with haughtiness, as if we had made ourselves to differ.

Article 16. But as man by the fall did not cease to be a creature, endowed with understanding and will, nor did sin which pervaded the whole race of mankind, deprive him of the human nature, but brought upon him depravity and spiritual death; so also this grace of regeneration does not treat men as senseless stocks and blocks, nor take away their will and its properties, neither does violence thereto; but spiritually quickens, heals, corrects, and at the same time sweetly and powerfully bends it; that where carnal rebellion and resistance formerly prevailed, a ready and sincere spiritual obedience begins to reign; in which the true and spiritual restoration and freedom of our will consist. Wherefore unless the admirable author of every good work wrought in us, man could have no hope of recovering from his fall by his own free will, by the abuse of which, in a state of innocence, he plunged himself into ruin.

Article 17. As the almighty operation of God, whereby he prolongs and supports this our natural life, does not exclude, but requires the use of means, by which God of his infinite mercy and goodness hath chosen to exert his influence, so also the before mentioned supernatural operation of God, by which we are regenerated, in no wise excludes, or subverts the use of the gospel, which the most wise God has ordained to be the seed of regeneration, and food of the soul. Wherefore, as the apostles, and teachers who succeeded them, piously instructed the people concerning this grace of God, to his glory, and the abasement of all pride, and in the meantime, however, neglected not to keep them by the sacred precepts of the gospel in the exercise of the Word, sacraments and discipline; so even to this day, be it far from either instructors or instructed to presume to tempt God in the church by separating what he of his good pleasure hath most intimately joined together. For grace is conferred by means of admonitions; and the more readily we perform our duty, the more eminent usually is this blessing of God working in us, and the more directly is his work advanced; to whom alone all the glory both of means, and of their saving fruit and efficacy is forever due. Amen.

* * *

Rejection of Errors

The true doctrine having been explained, the Synod rejects the errors of those:

I. Who teach: That it cannot properly be said, that original sin in itself suffices to condemn the whole human race, or to deserve temporal and eternal punishment. For these contradict the Apostle, who declares: "Therefore as through one man sin entered into the world, and death through sin, and so death passed unto all men, for that all sinned," Romans 5:12. And: "The judgment came of one unto condemnation," Romans 5:16. And: "The wages of sin is death," Romans 6:23.

II. Who teach: That the spiritual gifts, or the good qualities and virtues, such as: goodness, holiness, righteousness, could not belong to the will of man when he was first created, and that these, therefore, could not have been separated therefrom in the fall. For such is contrary to the description of the image of God, which the Apostle gives in Ephesians 4:24, where he declares that it consists in righteousness and holiness, which undoubtedly belong to the will.

III. Who teach: That in spiritual death the spiritual gifts are not separate from the will of man, since the will in itself has never been corrupted, but only hindered through the darkness of the understanding and the irregularity of the affections; and that, these hindrances having been removed, the will can then bring into operation its native powers, that is, that the will of itself is able to will and to choose, or not to will and not to choose, all manner of good which may be presented to it. This is an innovation and an error and tends to elevate the powers of the free will, contrary to the declaration of the Prophet: "The heart is deceitful above all things, and it is exceedingly corrupt," Jeremiah 17:9; and of the Apostle: "Among whom (sons of disobedience) we also all once lived in the lusts of the flesh, doing the desires of the flesh and of the mind," Ephesians 2:3.

IV. Who teach: That the unregenerate man is not really nor utterly dead in sin, nor destitute of all powers unto spiritual good, but that he can yet hunger and thirst after righteousness and life, and offer the sacrifice of a contrite and broken spirit, which is pleasing to God. For these are contrary to the express testimony of Scripture. "Ye were dead through trespasses and sins," Ephesians 2:1, 5; and: "Every imagination of the thought of his heart are only evil continually," Genesis 6:5; 8:21.

Moreover, to hunger and thirst after deliverance from misery, and after life, and to offer unto God the sacrifice of a broken spirit, is peculiar to the regenerate and those that are called blessed, Psalm 51:10, 19; Matthew 5:6.

V. Who teach: That the corrupt and natural man can so well use the common grace (by which they understand the light of nature), or the gifts still left him after the fall, that he can gradually gain by their good use a greater, namely, the evangelical or saving grace and salvation itself. And that in this way God on his part shows himself ready to reveal Christ unto all men, since he applies to all sufficiently and efficiently the means necessary to conversion. For the experience of all ages and the Scriptures do both testify that this is untrue. "He showeth his Word unto Jacob, his statues and his ordinances unto Israel. He hath not dealt so with any nation: and as for his ordinances they have not known them," Psalm 147:19, 20. "Who in the generations gone by suffered all the nations to walk in their own way," Acts 14:16. And: "And they (Paul and his companions) having been forbidden of the Holy

Spirit to speak the word in Asia, and when they were come over against Mysia, they assayed to go into Bithynia, and the Spirit suffered them not," Acts 16:6, 7.

VI. Who teach: That in the true conversion of man, no new qualities, powers, or gifts can be infused by God into the will, and that therefore faith through which we are first converted, and because of which we are called believers, is not a quality or gift infused by God, but only an act of man, and that it can not be said to be a gift, except in respect of the power to attain to this faith. For thereby they contradict the Holy Scriptures, which declare that God infuses new qualities of faith, of obedience, and of the consciousness of his love into our hearts: "I will put my law in their inward parts, and in their hearts will I write it," Jeremiah 31:33. And: "I will pour water upon him that is thirsty, and streams upon the dry ground; I will pour my spirit upon thy seed," Isaiah 44:3. And: "The love of God hath been shed abroad in our hearts through the Holy Spirit which hath been given us," Romans 5:5. This is also repugnant to the continuous practice of the Church, which prays by the mouth of the Prophet thus: "Turn thou me, and I shall be turned," Jeremiah 31:18.

VII. Who teach: That the grace whereby we are converted to God is only a gentle advising, or (as others explain it), that this is the noblest manner of working in the conversion of man, and that this manner of working, which consists in advising, is most in harmony with man's nature; and that there is no reason why this advising grace alone should not be sufficient to make the natural man spiritual, indeed, that God does not produce the consent of the will except through this manner of advising; and that the power of the divine working, whereby it surpasses the working of Satan, consists in this, that God promises eternal, while Satan promises only temporal goods. But this is altogether Pelagian and contrary to the whole Scripture which, besides this, teaches another and far more powerful and divine manner of the Holy Spirit's working in the conversion of man, as in Ezekiel: "A new heart also will I give you, and a new spirit will I put within you; and I will take away the stony heart out of your flesh, and I will give you a heart of flesh," Ezekiel 36:26.

VIII. Who teach: That God in the regeneration of man does not use such powers of his omnipotence as potently and infallibly bend man's will to faith and conversion; but that all the works of grace having been accomplished, which God employs to convert man, man may yet so resist God and the Holy Spirit, when God intends man's regeneration and wills to regenerate him, and indeed that man often does so resist that he prevents entirely his regeneration, and that it therefore remains in man's power to be regenerated or not. For this is nothing less than the denial of all the efficiency of God's grace in our conversion, and the subjecting of the working of Almighty God to the will of man, which is contrary to the Apostles, who teach: "That we believe according to the working of the strength of his power," Ephesians 1:19. And: "That God fulfills every desire of goodness and every work of faith with power," 2 Thessalonians 1:11. And: "That his divine power hath given unto us all things that pertain unto life and godliness," 2 Peter 1:3.

IX. Who teach: That grace and free will are partial causes, which together work the beginning of conversion, and that grace, in order of working, does not precede the working of the will; that is, that God does not efficiently help the will of man unto conversion until the will of man moves and determines to do this. For the ancient Church has long ago condemned this doctrine of the Pelagians according to the words of the Apostle: "So then it is not of him that willeth, nor of him that runneth, but of God that hath mercy," Romans 9:16. Likewise: "For who maketh thee to differ? and what hast thou that thou didst not receive?" I Corinthians 4:7. And: "For it is God who worketh in you both to will and to work, for his good pleasure," Philippians 2:13.

Fifth Head of Doctrine

Of the Perseverance of the Saints

Article 1. Whom God calls, according to his purpose, to the communion of his Son, our Lord Jesus Christ, and regenerates by the Holy Spirit, he delivers also from the dominion and slavery of sin in this life; though not altogether from the body of sin, and from the infirmities of the flesh, so long as they continue in this world.

Article 2. Hence spring daily sins of infirmity, and hence spots adhere to the best works of the saints; which furnish them with constant matter for humiliation before God, and flying for refuge to Christ crucified; for mortifying the flesh more and more by the spirit of prayer, and by holy exercises of piety; and for pressing forward to the goal of perfection, till being at length delivered from this body of death, they are brought to reign with the Lamb of God in heaven.

Article 3. By reason of these remains of indwelling sin, and the temptations of sin and of the world, those who are converted could not persevere in a state of grace, if left to their own strength. But God is faithful, who having conferred grace, mercifully confirms, and powerfully preserves them herein, even to the end.

Article 4. Although the weakness of the flesh cannot prevail against the power of God, who confirms and preserves true believers in a state of grace, yet converts are not always so influenced and actuated by the Spirit of God, as not in some particular instances sinfully to deviate from the guidance of divine grace, so as to be seduced by, and to comply with the lusts of the flesh; they must, therefore, be constant in watching and in prayer, that they be not led into temptation. When these are neglected, they are not only liable to be drawn into great and heinous sins, by Satan, the world and the flesh, but sometimes by the righteous permission of God actually fall into these evils. This, the lamentable fall of David, Peter, and other saints described in Holy Scripture, demonstrates.

Article 5. By such enormous sins, however, they very highly offend God, incur a deadly guilt, grieve the Holy Spirit, interrupt the exercise of faith, very grievously wound their consciences, and sometimes lose the sense of God's favor, for a time, until on their returning into the right way of serious repentance, the light of God's fatherly countenance again shines upon them.

Article 6. But God, who is rich in mercy, according to his unchangeable purpose of election, does not wholly withdraw the Holy Spirit from his own people, even in their melancholy falls; nor suffers them to proceed so far as to lose the grace of adoption, and forfeit the state of justification, or to commit sins unto death; nor does he permit them to be totally deserted, and to plunge themselves into everlasting destruction.

Article 7. For in the first place, in these falls he preserves them in the incorruptible seed of regeneration from perishing, or being totally lost; and again, by his Word and Spirit, certainly and effectually renews them to repentance, to a sincere and godly sorrow for their sins, that they may seek and obtain remission in the blood of the Mediator, may again experience the favor of a reconciled God, through faith adore his mercies, and henceforward more diligently work out their own salvation with fear and trembling.

Article 8. Thus, it is not in consequence of their own merits, or strength, but of God's free mercy, that they do not totally fall from faith and grace, nor continue and perish finally in their backslidings; which, with respect to themselves, is not only possible, but would undoubtedly happen; but with respect to God, it is utterly impossible, since his counsel cannot be changed, nor his promise fail, neither can the call according to his purpose be revoked, nor the merit, intercession and preservation of Christ be rendered ineffectual, nor the sealing of the Holy Spirit be frustrated or obliterated.

Article 9. Of this preservation of the elect to salvation, and of their perseverance in the faith, true believers for themselves may and ought to obtain assurance according to the measure of their faith, whereby they arrive at the certain persuasion, that they ever will continue true and living members of the church; and that they experience forgiveness of sins, and will at last inherit eternal life.

Article 10. This assurance, however, is not produced by any peculiar revelation contrary to, or independent of the Word of God; but springs from faith in God's promises, which he has most abundantly revealed in his Word for our comfort; from the testimony of the Holy Spirit, witnessing with our spirit, that we are children and heirs of God, Romans 8:16; and lastly, from a serious and holy desire to preserve a good conscience, and to perform good works. And if the elect of God were deprived of this solid comfort, that they shall finally obtain the victory, and of this infallible pledge or earnest of eternal glory, they would be of all men the most miserable.

Article 11. The Scripture moreover testifies that believers in this life have to struggle with various carnal doubts, and that under grievous temptations they are not always sensible of this full assurance of faith and certainty of persevering. But God, who is the Father of all consolation, does not suffer them to be tempted above that they are able, but will with the temptation also make a way to escape, that they may be able to bear it, 1 Corinthians 10:13, and by the Holy Spirit again inspires them with the comfortable assurance of persevering.

Article 12. This certainty of perseverance, however, is so far from exciting in believers a spirit of pride, or of rendering them carnally secure, that on the contrary, it is the real source of humility, filial reverence, true piety, patience in every tribulation, fervent prayers, constancy in suffering, and in confessing the truth, and of solid rejoicing in God: so that the consideration of this benefit should serve as an incentive to the serious and constant practice of gratitude and good works, as appears from the testimonies of Scripture, and the examples of the saints.

Article 13. Neither does renewed confidence or persevering produce licentiousness, or a disregard to piety in those who are recovering from backsliding; but it renders them much more careful and solicitous to continue in the ways of the Lord, which he hath ordained, that they who walk therein may maintain an assurance of persevering, lest by abusing his fatherly kindness, God should turn away his gracious countenance from them, to behold which is to the godly dearer than life: the withdrawing thereof is more bitter than death, and they in consequence hereof should fall into more grievous torments of conscience.

Article 14. And as it hath pleased God, by the preaching of the gospel, to begin this work of grace in us, so he preserves, continues, and perfects it by the hearing and reading of his Word, by meditation thereon, and by the exhortations, threatenings, and promises thereof, as well as by the use of the sacraments.

Article 15. The carnal mind is unable to comprehend this doctrine of the perseverance of the saints, and the certainty thereof; which God hath most abundantly revealed in his Word, for the glory of his name, and the consolation of pious souls, and which he impresses upon the hearts of the faithful. Satan abhors it; the world ridicules it; the ignorant and hypocrite abuse, and heretics oppose it; but the spouse of Christ hath always most tenderly loved and constantly defended it, as an inestimable treasure; and

God, against whom neither counsel nor strength can prevail, will dispose her to continue this conduct to the end. Now, to this one God, Father, Son, and Holy Spirit, be honor and glory, forever. AMEN.

* * *

Rejection of Errors

The true doctrine having been explained, the Synod rejects the errors of those:

I. Who teach: That the perseverance of the true believers is not a fruit of election, or a gift of God, gained by the death of Christ, but a condition of the new covenant, which (as they declare) man before his decisive election and justification must fulfill through his free will. For the Holy Scripture testifies that this follows out of election, and is given the elect in virtue of the death, the resurrection and intercession of Christ: "But the elect obtained it and the rest were hardened," Romans 11:7. Likewise: "He that spared not his own Son, but delivered him up for us all, how shall he not also with him freely give us all things? Who shall lay anything to the charge of God's elect? It is God that justifieth; who is he that condemneth? It is Christ Jesus that died, yea rather, that was raised from the dead, who is at the right hand of God, who also maketh intercession for us. Who shall separate us from the love of Christ?" Romans 8:32–35.

II. Who teach: That God does indeed provide the believer with sufficient powers to persevere, and is ever ready to preserve these in him, if he will do his duty; but that though all things, which are necessary to persevere in faith and which God will use to preserve faith, are made use of, it even then ever depends on the pleasure of the will whether it will persevere or not. For this idea contains an outspoken Pelagianism, and while it would make men free, it makes them robbers of God's honor, contrary to the prevailing agreement of the evangelical doctrine, which takes from man all cause of boasting, and ascribes all the praise for this favor to the grace of God alone; and contrary to the Apostle, who declares: "That it is God, who shall also confirm you unto the end, that ye be unreprovable in the day of our Lord Jesus Christ," 1 Corinthians 1:8.

III. Who teach: That the true believers and regenerate not only can fall from justifying faith and likewise from grace and salvation wholly and to the end, but indeed often do fall from this and are lost forever. For this conception makes powerless the grace, justification, regeneration, and continued keeping by Christ, contrary to the expressed words of the Apostle Paul: "That while we were yet sinners Christ died for us. Much more then, being justified by his blood, shall we be saved from the wrath of God through him," Romans 5:8, 9. And contrary to the Apostle John: "Whosoever is begotten of God doeth no sin, because his seed abideth in him; and he can not sin, because he is begotten of God," 1 John 3:9. And also contrary to the words of Jesus Christ: "I give unto them eternal life; and they shall never perish, and no one shall snatch them out of my hand. My Father who hath given them to me, is greater than all; and no one is able to snatch them out of the Father's hand," John 10:28, 29.

IV. Who teach: That true believers and regenerate can sin the sin unto death or against the Holy Spirit. Since the same Apostle

John, after having spoken in the fifth chapter of his first epistle, vss. 16 and 17, of those who sin unto death and having forbidden to pray for them, immediately adds to this in vs. 18: "We know that whosoever is begotten of God sinneth not (meaning a sin of that character), but he that is begotten of God keepeth himself, and the evil one toucheth him not," 1 John 5:18.

V. Who teach: That without a special revelation we can have no certainty of future perseverance in this life. For by this doctrine the sure comfort of all believers is taken away in this life, and the doubts of the papist are again introduced into the church, while the Holy Scriptures constantly deduce this assurance, not from a special and extraordinary revelation, but from the marks proper to the children of God and from the constant promises of God. So especially the Apostle Paul: "No creature shall be able to separate us from the love of God, which is in Christ Jesus our Lord," Romans 8:39. And John declares: "And he that keepeth his commandments abideth in him, and he in him. And hereby we know that he abideth in us, by the Spirit which he gave us," 1 John 3:24.

VI. Who teach: That the doctrine of the certainty of perseverance and of salvation from its own character and nature is a cause of indolence and is injurious to godliness, good morals, prayers, and other holy exercises, but that on the contrary it is praiseworthy to doubt. For these show that they do not know the power of divine grace and the working of the indwelling Holy Spirit. And they contradict the Apostle John, who teaches the opposite with express words in his first epistle: "Beloved, now are we the children of God, and it is not yet made manifest what we shall be. We know that, if he shall be manifested, we shall be like him, for we shall see him even as he is. And every one that hath this hope in him purifieth himself, even as he is pure," 1 John 3:2, 3. Furthermore, these are contradicted by the example of the saints, both of the Old and New Testament, who though they were assured of their perseverance and salvation, were nevertheless constant in prayers and other exercises of godliness.

VII. Who teach: That the faith of those, who believe for a time, does not differ from justifying and saving faith except only in duration. For Christ himself, in Matthew 13:20; Luke 8:13, and in other places, evidently notes, besides this duration, a threefold difference between those who believe only for a time and true believers, when he declares that the former receive the seed in stony ground, but the latter in the good ground or heart; that the former are without root, but that the latter have a firm root; that the former are without fruit, but that the latter bring forth their fruit in various measure, with constancy and steadfastness.

VIII. Who teach: That it is not absurd that one having lost his first regeneration, is again and even often born anew. For these deny by this doctrine the incorruptibleness of the seed of God, whereby we are born again. Contrary to the testimony of the Apostle Peter: "Having been begotten again, not of corruptible seed, but of incorruptible," 1 Peter 1:23.

IX. Who teach: That Christ has in no place prayed that believers should infallibly continue in faith. For they contradict Christ himself, who says: "I have prayed for thee (Simon), that thy faith fail not," Luke 22:32; and the Evangelist John, who declares, that Christ has not prayed for the Apostles only, but also for those who through their word would believer: "Holy Father, keep them in thy name," and: "I pray not that thou shouldest take them out of the world, but that thou shouldest keep them from the evil one," John 17:11, 15, 20.

Conclusion

And this is the perspicuous, simple, and ingenious declaration of the orthodox doctrine respecting the five articles which have been controverted in the Belgic churches; and the rejection of the errors, with which they have for some time been troubled. This doctrine, the Synod judges to be drawn from the Word of God, and to be agreeable to the confessions of the Reformed churches. Whence it clearly appears, that some whom such conduct by no means became, have violated all truth, equity, and charity, in wishing to persuade the public.

"That the doctrine of the Reformed churches concerning predestination, and the points annexed to it, by its own genius and necessary tendency, leads off the minds of men from all piety and religion; that it is an opiate administered by the flesh and by the devil, and the stronghold of Satan, where he lies in wait for all; and from which he wounds multitudes, and mortally strikes through many with the darts both of despair and security; that it makes God the author of sin, unjust, tyrannical, hypocritical; that it is nothing more than interpolated Stoicism, Manicheism, Libertinism, Turcism; that it renders men carnally secure, since they are persuaded by it that nothing can hinder the salvation of the elect, let them live as they please; and therefore, that they may safely perpetrate every species of the most atrocious crimes; and that, if the reprobate should even perform truly all the works of the saints, their obedience would not in the least contribute to their salvation; that the same doctrine teaches, that God, by a mere arbitrary act of his will, without the least respect or view to sin, has predestinated the greatest part of the world to eternal damnation; and, has created them for this very purpose; that in the same manner in which the election is the fountain and cause of faith and good works, reprobation is the cause of unbelief and impiety; that many children of the faithful are torn, guiltless, from their mothers' breasts, and tyrannically plunged into hell; so that, neither baptism, nor the prayers of the Church at their baptism, can at all profit by them;" and many other things of the same kind, which the Reformed Churches not only do not acknowledge, but even detest with their whole soul.

Wherefore, this Synod of Dort, in the name of the Lord, conjures as many as piously call upon the name of our Savior Jesus Christ, to judge of the faith of the Reformed Churches, not from the calumnies, which, on every side, are heaped upon it; nor from the private expressions of a few among ancient and modern teachers, often dishonestly quoted, or corrupted, and wrested to a meaning quite foreign to their intention; but from the public confessions of the Churches themselves, and from the declaration of the orthodox doctrine, confirmed by the unanimous consent of all and each of the members of the whole Synod.

Moreover, the Synod warns calumniators themselves, to consider the terrible judgment of God which awaits them, for bearing false witness against the confessions of so many Churches, for distressing the consciences of the weak; and for laboring to render suspected the society of the truly faithful.

Finally, this Synod exhorts all their brethren in the gospel of Christ, to conduct themselves piously and religiously in handling this doctrine, both in the universities and churches; to direct it, as well in discourse, as in writing, to the glory of the Divine Name, to holiness of life, and to the consolation of afflicted souls; to regulate, by the Scripture, according to the analogy of faith, not only their sentiments, but also their language; and, to abstain from all those phrases which exceed the limits necessary to be observed in ascertaining the genuine sense of the holy Scriptures; and may furnish insolent sophists with a just pretext for violently assailing, or even vilifying, the doctrine of the Reformed Churches.

May Jesus Christ, the Son of God, who, seated at the Father's right hand, gives gifts to men, sanctify us in the truth, bring to the truth those who err, shut the mouths of the calumniators of sound doctrine, and endue the faithful minister of his Word with the spirit of wisdom and discretion, that all their discourses may tend to the glory of God, and the edification of those who hear them. AMEN.

* * *

That this is our faith and decision we certify by subscribing our names.

(Here follow the names, not only of President, Assistant President, and Secretaries of the Synod, and of the Professors of Theology in the Dutch Churches, but of all the Members who were deputed to Synod, as the representatives of their respective Churches, that is, of the Delegates from Great Britain, the Electoral Palatinate, Hessia, Switzerland, Wetteraw, the Republic and Church of Geneva, The Republic and Church of Bremen, The Republic and Church of Emden, The Duchy of Gelderland and of Zutphen, South Holland, North Holland, Zeeland, The Province of Utrecht, Friesland, Transylvania, The State of Groningen and Omland, Drent, The French Churches.)

www.ingramcontent.com/pod-product-compliance
Ingram Content Group UK Ltd.
Pitfield, Milton Keynes, MK11 3LW, UK
UKHW022003190726
13853UKWH00004B/1698

9 798986 509068